Life After My Moth

Tashi Hansen du Toit was 15 years old when her mother, Karen, suffered a severe haemorrhagic stroke which left her with multiple physical and cognitive impairments. This beautifully written and poignant account tells Tashi's story from the first moments after her mother's stroke, following her and her family through the experience of her mother's hospitalisation and rehabilitation. Tashi offers a rare glimpse into the impact of her mother's stroke on her family and on her life as a teenager as she juggles the stresses and demands of family, school, and friends alongside coping with her mother's brain injury. As she describes how she is learning to cope with her unresolved grief three years on, she provides hope, perspective, and insight on how to work towards growth and acceptance despite the catastrophe of a parent's stroke.

Presenting the rarely heard adolescent perspective on parental brain injury, Tashi's moving story also features Karen's account as she comes to terms with her experience. This authentic book offers great support to others, particularly teenagers, who may be going through a similar experience. It is also valuable reading for those working in brain injury services and the education system, and for any professional or student involved in neurorehabilitation or supporting families of parents with brain injury.

Tashi Hansen du Toit is the daughter of Karen Hansen and Pieter du Toit. In 2018, while Tashi was completing her GCSE exams, her mother had a stroke. After completing her A-levels in 2021, Tashi is taking a gap year.

Pieter du Toit is the father of Tashi Hansen du Toit and husband of Karen Hansen. Pieter works as a clinical psychologist specialising in neuropsychology at the Oliver Zangwill Centre for Neuropsychological Rehabilitation in Ely, UK and in private practice in Cambridge, UK.

After Brain Injury: Survivor Stories

This new series of books is aimed at those who have suffered a brain injury, and their families and carers. Each book focuses on a different condition, such as face blindness, amnesia and neglect, or diagnosis, such as encephalitis and locked-in syndrome, resulting from brain injury. Readers will learn about life before the brain injury, the early days of diagnosis, the effects of the brain injury, the process of rehabilitation, and life now. Alongside this personal perspective, professional commentary is also provided by a specialist in neuropsychological rehabilitation, making the books relevant for professionals working in rehabilitation such as psychologists, speech and language therapists, occupational therapists, social workers and rehabilitation doctors. They will also appeal to clinical psychology trainees and undergraduate and graduate students in neuropsychology, rehabilitation science, and related courses who value the case study approach.

With this series, we also hope to help expand awareness of brain injury and its consequences. The World Health Organization has recently acknowledged the need to raise the profile of mental health issues (with the WHO Mental Health Action Plan 2013-20) and we believe there needs to be a similar focus on psychological, neurological and behavioural issues caused by brain disorder, and a deeper understanding of the importance of rehabilitation support. Giving a voice to these survivors of brain injury is a step in the right direction.

Series Editor: Barbara A. Wilson

Published titles:

Reconstructing Identity After Brain Injury
A Search for Hope and Optimism After Maxillofacial and Neurosurgery
Stijn Geerinck

For more information about this series, please visit: https://www.routledge.com/After-Brain-Injury-Survivor-Stories/book-series/ABI

Life After My Mother's Stroke

A Teenage Take on How to Cope

Tashi Hansen du Toit and Pieter du Toit

Routledge
Taylor & Francis Group

LONDON AND NEW YORK

Cover image: © Tashi Hansen du Toit

First published 2022
by Routledge
4 Park Square, Milton Park, Abingdon, Oxon OX14 4RN

and by Routledge
605 Third Avenue, New York, NY 10158

Routledge is an imprint of the Taylor & Francis Group, an informa business

© 2022 Tashi Hansen du Toit and Pieter du Toit

The right of Tashi Hansen du Toit and Pieter du Toit to be identified as authors of this work has been asserted in accordance with sections 77 and 78 of the Copyright, Designs and Patents Act 1988.

British Library Cataloguing-in-Publication Data
A catalogue record for this book is available from the British Library

Library of Congress Cataloging-in-Publication Data
A catalog record has been requested for this book

ISBN: 978-0-367-77498-1 (hbk)
ISBN: 978-0-367-77500-1 (pbk)
ISBN: 978-1-003-17167-6 (ebk)

DOI: 10.4324/9781003171676

Typeset in Times New Roman
by Taylor & Francis Books

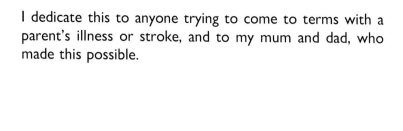

I dedicate this to anyone trying to come to terms with a parent's illness or stroke, and to my mum and dad, who made this possible.

Contents

Figures

Foreword

Survivors' Stories is a series written by those who have suffered brain injury and their families and carers. Each book focuses on a different condition, such as face blindness, amnesia and neglect, or diagnosis, such as encephalitis and locked-in syndrome resulting from brain injury. This is the first book in the Survivors' Stories series that has been written by a teenager. Her mother had a severe stroke in 2018 when Tashi Hansen du Toit was 15 years old. Everyone involved in the production of this book has expressed astonishment at its maturity, its depth of perception, and extraordinary clarity of expression. Tashi describes with great poignancy and sensitivity how she dealt with the immediate problem, how she coped with the aftermath, how she helped her little sister, the difficulties involved in continuing her education, and how she struggled with family, friends and professionals to unravel many of the challenges facing her. Her writing is simply admirable and reflects an enormous talent that will surely continue to flourish in what looks likely to be a gifted future in writing.

I became involved in the story as I worked with Tashi's father, Pieter, with whom I shared an office. Pieter of course was deeply and devastatingly caught up in the subsequent personal and emotional problems of his wife's brain injury as well as inevitably having a professional outlook. I had also previously worked with patients with a disorder of consciousness (DOC) and, having assessed such patients, as well as those just emerging from a DOC, I went to see Karen in Addenbrooke's Hospital in Cambridge with Pieter to administer a test for people with a severe brain injury. Another area which strongly resonates is the point Tashi makes in the book that it is hard to grieve for someone who is living. This is addressed in an editorial of mine about the similarities and differences between bereaved families and families of someone with a severe brain injury (Wilson 2020). Tashi's godmother, mentioned several times in the book, is Jill Winegardner, a close friend of mine, so there were definitely a number of reasons connecting me to this story and of course making it an essential part of the Brain Injury Survivors' Stories. However, initial readership by a number of professionals involved in the series has led us to consider giving Tashi's account a wider audience by offering it to the general population. It certainly deserves it!

Reference

Wilson B. A. (2020). Similarities and differences between bereaved parents and parents of someone with a severe brain injury: What can we do to help? Published online *Neuropsychological Rehabilitation*.

Chapter 1

My mother's stroke

I hear my name – Mum is calling me. When I come downstairs, I see her lying in bed: "Mum, do you want me to get you Ribena?". She sometimes gets low blood sugar because of her diabetes, and I have learned to be quick when it comes to offering her a sugary drink. "No, it's not low blood sugar. We need to call your dad. Something is wrong". Her eyes are open, but as I call my dad, the left corner of her mouth starts to droop and her speech is slurred, her tongue getting caught in her teeth: "I heard a pop. I have a headache... a really bad one...".

"Dad, there's something wrong with Mum... I don't think it's her blood sugar". My dad is still at work. He tells me he's going to call emergency services while I stay on the line with Mum. I can hear the 999 operator in the background as my dad juggles the two calls. He tells me they will call me and he's going to come home. He says the ambulance will be with us soon. My little sister, Léa, is watching *Kung Fu Panda* downstairs. I hold Mum's hand; she seems calm, but I can sense that she is scared: "I love you

DOI: 10.4324/9781003171676-1

Mum," I keep saying. I tell her – I lie – that she's going to be OK and that the ambulance will be with us soon. She manages to tell me to pack an overnight bag for her. After some minutes, someone's at the front door. I leave Mum and rush – it's a man in green scrubs and a car marked "Ambulance" is parked in our driveway. I bring him upstairs… the tune from *Kung Fu Panda* plays in the background….

"How are you feeling?" he asks. We can't understand what she says – maybe "Not so good". "Lift up your arms for me Karen…". He has a big dipper tattoo on his forearm and greasy hair in a headband. The man keeps saying her name as if he's talking to someone who is drunk or something. She tries to lift her hands but her left arm doesn't move. He turns to me: "I'm going to call the ambulance and we'll take her to Addenbrooke's. It's good you called. They'll be here soon". I offer him coffee, but he's not interested.

When the doorbell rings again, I let in two paramedics – this time a woman with a ponytail and an older guy, who tells me his name is Andy. I'm vaguely aware that my little sister is watching another *Kung Fu Panda* episode in the living room. I take the paramedics upstairs. They take Mum's blood pressure and blood sugars. When they've run their tests, I ask whether Mum's had a stroke. "We're not allowed to say," says Andy. The stairway is too narrow for a stretcher, so the woman fetches what looks like a chair. They strap Mum into the chair. She starts vomiting as they try to carry the chair down the stairs. She twitches. I've never seen anyone have a seizure, but it reminds me of when Somba, our Tibetan terrier, had a fit – his paws were outstretched and his head lolled to one side, like a lopsided Sphinx. My dad raced him to the after-hours vet that day and as soon as he got to the vets, the dog was fine.

Somba is getting in the way, and I make an excuse for him, but greasy hair guy fusses over him. They struggle to get Mum downstairs and then she's in the ambulance and they're off to the hospital. Everything is quiet – back to normal. *Kung Fu Panda* seems endless. I tell my little sister: "Mummy has gone to hospital, but the people are taking really good care of her".

"Is she having a baby?" she asks, her eyes still glued to her show.

"No, she's just a little bit ill right now," I say. I think everyday thoughts: When will Dad be home? Should I make dinner now? Mum left a cup with some coffee still in it upstairs. The bed is messed up and some ECG pads are lying around on the floor, where I leave them.

Our neighbour comes over and asks why there was an ambulance. I explain that my mum has had a stroke. She comes in and offers to look after my sister until my dad comes home. She looks worried. Inside I feel really scared. I act confident, asking her whether she wants coffee. I tell her: "Everything is probably going to be OK", but I don't think it will be and by her expression, neither does she. She sits with my sister and they seem lost in conversation about different kids' shows. This is the first moment I don't feel I need to do anything. I message my best friend:

"My mums in hospital"

"Shit. What happened? Are you okay?
Is she okay?"

"Idk.. i think she's had a stroke- the ambulance j left"
"My dad's coming home now he'll be here in like 15 mins"

"Do you want me to come over?
I can look after your sister of something"

"Nah it's okay our neighbour has come over
they're j watching a movie lol"

A key rattles in the front door, it's my dad. He rushes in with his folding bike, scraping it against the wall. A colleague had to bring him home because the trains were running late when I called him at work. He's in action mode. No time for hugs.

"Pack a bag for Mum – toothbrush that kind of thing".

As he walks through to the kitchen, I wonder what Mom will actually need – phone charger, toothbrush, underwear, clothes? Pyjamas? She was always the one who packed our stuff on camping trips and holidays. I rush upstairs – my dad seems in a hurry, so no time to waste.

"Tashi, do you want to come with me?", my dad asks me. I can see that he's wondering whether this is a good idea, but his colleague has offered to stay with Léa until we come back. "Sure". Is it a good idea? Could I actually have said no? We drive to the hospital – it's really close, but it seems to take hours to find parking. People with flowers, packages for patients… a blur. We go straight to A&E as my dad thinks that would be the most likely place that Mum would be. Everyone and everything seems to be in our way. I catch my breath as we make our way deep into the backrooms of A&E, pass all the people waiting. A plump-cheeked nurse who seems just a few years older than me tells us: "I'll check to see which room she's in. Just wait here". Waiting here means sitting next to a boy and his mother; he's about the age of my sister and he cries quietly – his mother softly whispering to him and holding him. A loud man complains about having to wait so long – he's hurt his ribs or something. Nothing around us seems as serious as having a stroke…. The nurse tells the man to go home and take some paracetamol. He's not happy with this: "Why don't I need an X-ray?". He leaves in the end after the woman with him drags him off.

Finally, a doctor comes and leads us to the inner parts of A&E. Once we get there, I'm surprised to see Mum lying on a bed with nothing much happening. I recall those posters – F.A.S.T. or something – doesn't time matter when you've had a stroke? Like the nurse at the front desk, the doctor seems young too – he introduces himself again and says he's a junior doctor. My dad tries to find out more about Mum, but he doesn't give much. There's no one actually doing anything to Mum and this doesn't make much sense to me after the rush back at home to get her to the hospital.

"Hi Mum..." – I hold her hand. Her speech is slurred and her eyes open and close. She asks: "Is... Léa here?". I tell her my little sister is at home and that she's being looked after by Dad's colleague. She calms down a little, but then she begins to choke. She retches and my dad rushes over. No one else seems to care much about this. There is no nurse or doctor around and my dad and I hold my mum forwards. I hold a little cardboard bowl for her to vomit into. At times it sounds as if she's choking. My dad's very upset and tries to put on his calm voice when he asks a nurse to come over and help. The nurse helps me as Mum keeps retching. Mum looks much worse than earlier as she says: "I love my mummy...". She has never called my *mormor* (the Danish for mother's mother) that. Dad manages to call my grandmother in Canada, but my mum is unable to talk much.

The wait is endless. Eventually, an annoyed sounding doctor with an eastern European accent asks why my mum has not yet had a scan. She seems irritated with the junior doctors who scuttle away to arrange things. Mum is taken away for a brain scan. This at least seems as if something is actually happening, instead of just letting things take their course. We sit there, surrounded by other patients and a surprising lack of urgency or activity. We're told that it's busy, but it doesn't seem as if a lot is happening around us. I hear the beeping of many machines; it's also very bright in here – nowhere for illness to hide....

They bring mum back but she's not saying much now – she seems unconscious. The doctors talk to my dad and I listen in. I can hear what's going on but can see that they don't want to upset me. But when my dad goes off to the toilet, the nurses come and go. Some talk to me as if I'm an adult, others ask me questions as if I'm a twelve-year-old: "You OK honey? What's your favourite animal? I've got a sticker!" – that kind of thing. Finally, the junior doctor tells us what they know:

> Karen has had a severe haemorrhagic stroke in her lower hypothalamus, we are going to do surgery to drain the blood but it will take a number of hours. We want to find out what caused the stroke.... There's something odd about this stranger calling my mother 'Karen'.

They wheel Mum off and we leave. Both Dad and I hesitate. It feels like we should stick around indefinitely to make sure Mum doesn't get overlooked as she did when she first arrived. What would have happened if we weren't there to help her upright whenever she retched? As we're walking back to the car, everything seems unreal. People eating fast food in the concourse; buying groceries at M&S. We drive home in silence – there's nothing much to say. It's late when we get home. My sister is wired – like she's had too much sugar.

"Where is Mummy?"

"She's in hospital for now," my dad says. She accepts this as answer enough. No further questions. She must be tired. He doesn't say that she's going to be OK, because it's clear to us that she won't be for a long time. He takes her off to bed. I think this is the latest she's ever been up. I am too tired to sleep. Outside I hear my visitor cat miaowing and I let him into the house. It's a quick bowl of milk for him. I'm too tired to give him much attention, but it feels good to press him against me. He looks shocked when I let him out too soon for his liking.

I'm so tired as I go up to my room. I fall onto my bed and hear the padding footsteps of my dog coming to see me – maybe he can smell the cat. I wonder what he thinks is happening. How could a dog even begin to understand this kind of stuff? My phone is buzzing incessantly, "Word's gotten out" I muse…everyone probably wants to help, wants to know if I'm "OK". What could I say? I put my phone on airplane mode – people are an issue for tomorrow.

I try to sleep, comforted by the heavy breathing of the dog at the foot of my bed and rain on the roof. I can see the red light blinking on the incinerator at the hospital – easy to spot in this flat city. There is no comfort in knowing: This is where Mum is tonight.

Just this morning, Mum had taken us to the dentist. Something which should have filled my little sister and me with dread, somehow it became fun with Mum as we sang along to the radio. She knew the songs I liked and the ones I pretended not to like anymore but still did. I have no one to sing with now. Too tired to sing anyway.

Today seems just as rushed as yesterday, but we don't seem to get far. It's 11 by the time we go for a walk with the dog and I've put my little sister's hair in panda bunches to make her smile. Everything takes forever to do. I wonder whether we're either too tired or too scared to set off early to the hospital. On the walk we find one stray daffodil – my dad makes a big deal of this, pointing out how odd this is for October. He's trying to distract us. Every time Léa sees any flower, she exclaims: "We'll give them to Mum!". We don't. It's difficult to explain to her that flowers do not belong in the part of the hospital where Mum is. I wonder about that: Why don't they? I picture nurses and doctors trying to resuscitate someone and having to fend off bouquets of flowers. No, surely that can't be the reason? Infection risk? Mosquitoes? Allergies?

I sleep-walk out of the car park on the way to the main entrance of the hospital. Léa tugs at my hand – she makes a game of jumping onto huge concrete bollards as we walk towards the hospital. Her excitement seems out of place, but I can feel that she's nervous underneath it all. Making the best of it. I can see that Dad wants to say something like: "Be careful!". He doesn't. How badly can things go wrong in comparison to Mum's stroke? Mum always lets me climb things – trees, walls – confident that nothing will really go wrong and if it did, that I'd be able to handle it.

I show Léa a life-sized cut-out of a scary looking flu virus at the reception while my dad tries to find out where Mum is. My sister loves the virus. The whole trip to the hospital suddenly seems much more exciting to her, as if we're going to be encountering all sorts of funny looking and essentially harmless monsters during our visit. And it really does feel like a labyrinth – the hospital. Either we're tired or it's been designed by someone with no sense of direction or it's a bit of both. I once heard my parents talking about someone they knew who actually got misplaced in the same hospital on the way to an operating room and wonder if the same thing can happen to Mum. Or to us.

The intercom buzzes. We're at the door of the NCCU. I fiddle while Dad presses the buzzer over and over – too hard. "Don't keep pressing the button, be more patient" would be what he normally tells me if I do this. He worries about these things – don't want to bother them, but wants to get in. My little sister distracts herself by jabbing her fingers at the staff photos on a notice board: "Boy, girl, girl, girl". Finally, a voice chirps and we're in. No greetings. Nurses and doctors everywhere. Surprisingly quiet really. Every single bed is full of someone; someone's dad, someone's mum… mostly greyer than my mum. There are wires everywhere and nurses in green fatigues waging war against death. Or something. Where is she… where is she? All the patients actually do look so similar.

There she is… she's completely out of it. Comatose. Unaware. I've never seen her like this; not really. Maybe when we go camping or so I may catch sight of Mum sleeping. But she's a light sleeper really. Maybe because she's always had to be kind of aware of us. Maybe because she's always had to be aware of measuring her blood sugars – comes with type one diabetes. But this is different – she seems completely unresponsive, and also fragile. I can sense my dad and sister hesitating instead of rushing to her. The nurses have to encourage us to do every next step. Is it even OK to draw chairs up to her bed? Can I take her hand in mine? It's like we need to ask permission here: Mum seems to belong to them now.

Dad told me that it felt as if the hospital "owned" me when I was born almost two months prematurely and kept in the NICU (Neonatal Intensive Care Unit) in a "Tupperware container" (as he called the little see-through cots the babies were kept in). I've even seen pictures of me looking confused by all the stuff (black and white mobiles, photos of Mum and Dad) my dad kept putting up in the cot for me. I think it was my parents' way of "owning" me and I enjoyed their stories of how the nurses kept removing most of these things and my parents then replacing them. I wonder what kind of things we can do here to "own" Mum in a place where every person and every bed can look so similar at first glance.

I take Mum's hand and squeeze it. Still her hands, her nails. But colder and coiled with wires and blue with bruises on her wrist. "Hi Mum… we are all here". No response. My sister asks about the tube in her mouth and the machines. Actually, there really are tubes everywhere and the rails around the bed make her seem even more fragile. There are two purple marker stripes on her forehead – they kind of annoy me, but I suppose that they probably need them to line her up for something. But she still looks like Mum. There's a friendly, beard of a nurse, kind smiles – not too much – just right. He gives my sister a stethoscope and she can't believe her luck – something for her doctor's kit.

There's a little kitchen and resting room for relatives. Léa seems delighted to find it, complete with children's toys. It has a notice board. Someone has carefully crafted bubbles with two or three words in them. I read out loud with my sister: "Finally, please" "look after" "yourselves" "Getting enough" "rest, eating and" "drinking is" "crucial, Your" "Loved one needs" "you to be well" "coming days". They must have left the words "in the" out, so that "coming days" sound kind of scary. I can't help myself – my dad and I resort to humour when we're stressed, and I wonder what would happen if I rearranged the bubbles: "Getting enough drinking is crucial". I resist the urge, instead looking at a picture of a *PAT (therapy)* dog that may one day come and visit.

Later, we learn that Mum had surgery and that it went well and that she's "stable". What does that even mean? The kind of word you hear on the news. Stable good or stable bad? Never thought of that word much. Are we stable? Am I? She's not awake – she's stable. I run out of thoughts. Over time, we just tune out the background noise. It's actually quite calming here. We're with her. And not.

"I can't smell Mum's Mommy smell". Léa is leaning over Mum, sniffing her hands, her arms… all the way up to her head. She seems so intent on what she's doing, completely unaware of how loud she is. I barely talk, and if I did, my dad would probably tell me to be quieter. I look at Dad. He seems to be holding himself back. Maybe he's worrying that my sister will unplug one of those tubes protruding from Mum. He's not showing it to her. Instead, he tries to sound reassuring: "I'm sure it will come back… it's just the hospital smells," he says. She's not convinced. I feel annoyed at her: She's said what we're all worried about – in her little girl kind of a way. Is Mum still the same? How much will she still be herself? How different will she be? What will be lost and what will come back?

After sitting with Mum for a while, the nurses busy themselves with some procedure and we leave for the relative's room. My sister seems absolutely engrossed in one of those beads-on-a-wire games and she seems delighted with the toys. My dad seems equally delighted that there's tea and coffee and that he can help himself to as much as he likes. I think he just needs something to do and to accomplish in this place and making a cup of tea probably feels like the only constructive thing he can really do here. I can see how tired he is. Léa asks: "How many sleeps is Mum going to be here?". He asks her to count the beads on the toy. It keeps her busy, but she doesn't miss a bead as she counts up... "Thirty!". He tells her that Mum is going to be in hospital for at least as many days as the beads she has just counted. She looks at him with disbelief – one bead alone seems like a lot of sleeps. She wiggles her jaw and then stops playing with the beads altogether, frowning: "I don't know what to do!". Neither do I.

It's late afternoon before we have lunch. I'm starving. My dad asks us how we found the visit. I wonder what he's expecting us to say. I wonder whether this is some kind of psychologist thing – a debriefing of sorts because I am pretty sure all of us found the visit disconcerting in our own specific ways. I don't have anything to say – still processing I suppose. "I saw tubes there, tubes there and tubes there... tubes here and tubes right over there!" my sister exclaims. To be honest, I think that about sums it up. Léa seems annoyed at all the tubes and I try to explain to her that they're really all a very good thing and that they're probably all helping Mum in some way to get better. She does not seem convinced.

I feel like I am on autopilot as we go to the hospital again after lunch. Already, I don't know where time goes. When we get back to Neuro Critical Care Unit (NCCU), there's a ward round or something and we have to wait. In the waiting room, I make my way through a white booklet on different parts of the brain. It raises more questions for me and it seems unreal: A week ago, I really never gave the word "stroke" a second thought, or if I heard it, it sounded irrelevant to my family – something only very old people got, I thought. Actually, it may even have been something I only ever heard in phrases like: "I almost had a stroke" – I may even have said it myself once or twice. Never again.

My dad brings along a little green sketch book from the Tate Modern Museum for visitors to write something in. I don't actually think that she is allowed any other visitors in here – just close family. The book seems a bit hopeful and also out of place – even dangerous, like flowers, something that could get in the way of some kind of procedure. I write in it: "We love you, Mum!". What else can I write? I hold it for my sister to make a stickman and a scribbly dog. When she is done, Dad takes the book and leaves it on the bedside trolley, next to three of those little bowls – the same ones I used yesterday in A&E when she retched. One of them has a little tube of toothpaste and what looks like a child's toothbrush. My sister is delighted when she sees these as she thinks they're for her. How can these be for my mum? The idea of someone else brushing my mum's teeth seems really difficult to get my head around.

It's after Léa's bedtime when we get to the parking garage and we're delighted to see our old neighbours there! My dad arranged a quick meeting with them as they were planning to see Mum too. There's almost too much laughing all around, with Dad saying it feels like something out of a movie like the *Italian Job*. My sister can't believe her luck when she gets a gigantic Pooh Bear cushion. At home we eat pasta and I goof around eating a strand of pasta and tempting our dog to eat the other end, which he does, obligingly. It's like that scene from *Lady and the Tramp* and for a moment, I forget all about hospitals, tiredness and what seems like a million unread messages on my phone. There's still a bag full of Duke of Edinburgh (DofE) stuff in it and I am too scared of what may be mouldering in it and too tired to confront it tonight.

When I get to my room, I thought that I'd be sleeping as soon as I got into bed, but I'm actually too tired and that bag of DofE stuff stirred me up. It seems like a year or more ago, but I just returned from a three-day DofE trip with five of my closest friends. If Mum were here, or if Dad were not so busy with "dealing" with everything after Mum's stroke, I would have had a chat about the whole trip. But there's much I would not have said – even to my mum. All these thoughts are swarming in my head and it feels like they will just keep milling about until I can process all the stuff that happened. And this is what I needed to talk about to someone, but never do.

On the trip, my closest friend was having a really difficult time. I told Dad something about this, but only touched the surface. My friend had struggled with mental health issues and it was difficult for her to talk even to me during the trip. I felt that I had to keep her and everyone else happy, but it was actually so difficult, since everyone literally seemed to be walking off into different directions. I blame myself for my friend's difficulty in talking about what troubled her. Almost a year ago we had fallen into something like a relationship. She was always unsure of her sexual orientation and I was the only one she had ever mentioned this to. One night, we came back to our house after we'd been to the cinema and she slept over. After that night, we were essentially best friends with a shared secret: We would mess about after school, hidden in the branches of the huge tree in our school ground. We'd hold hands when our friends weren't watching, excited as much about the secrecy as at actually holding hands. And then she kept trying to open up about just how difficult she was finding life and I wasn't there for her. I just avoided it all as I sometimes do, because I had my own issues – or so it seemed to me. I guess I just didn't feel up to the task of looking after myself, let alone someone else.

So, we drifted apart. Still friends, but without the good morning texts or secret kisses. I guess it was the lack of closure or definition which really messed with us. Almost a year later, we kissed again – enough to mean something. But because of my history of not really being there for her (or trying to be there for everyone equally), during the DofE trip, she walked off in the middle of the night. Two hours later, I really started worrying about her, because I could see from a mile away that she struggled and that she needed me, but I was with my friends and enjoying myself. I just let her walk off. Stupid, selfish, hedonistic me. Eventually, my guilt and concern for her made me take a torch and blanket and go in search of her. We were camping near an old church and cemetery and I will never forget the sense of dread I had as I set out to find her; or the relief when I found her half an hour later. I feel a sense of guilt and just before sleeping, I think again: Stupid, selfish, hedonistic me.

Almost ironically, I pray – this second night without Mum in the house. I pray while just a week ago Mum and I had a conversation about God. She kept her cards close to her chest about religion and I'm still not all that sure what precisely she believes. But she was brought up Lutheran in Canada and her family are involved in the church. "Please, please, please – just let her live". I don't really know what to ask for or who I'm asking it from. If I had anything to give or any promises to make, I'd do it, but I can't think of anything. So, I leave it at that. Dad's song comes to mind. He kept listening all the time to this song by Regina Spector, called *Laughing with* or something. I sing the song tunelessly, my throat feels thick. She's right: No one laughs at God when they're in a hospital, I think. But I disagree with her, unless she's being ironic: I don't find God hilarious at all.

I wake up to the smell of pancakes. My sister is wearing a dark blue shark onesie and has already smeared Nutella thickly on some pancakes and her face. It seems like a normal, autumn break day. Only, Mum is not there. I feel as if we're trying out different ways of getting through the day. We go to a local park with the dog. He's delighted and runs around in figure eights with a stick in his mouth, making people smile. I put on his red bow tie earlier to cheer me up – he looks like a furry professor. When my sister and I work on building a den, a little robin observes us. We try following it to see whether it has a nest somewhere.

When we get home, our neighbour pops over and gives my dad some groceries they had bought for us. I can see my dad is tearful as he looks at the things they gave us – just the basics but just what we needed. When she leaves, my dad unpacks the bread, pasta sauce, apples, milk: "What's wrong with me? I wanted all these things but didn't even think of getting basics like this! We really needed this". My phone buzzes again – I feel like just deleting all my apps so that I don't constantly get reminded of everyone I know trying to get in touch with me. Probably not a good idea.

A smiley nurse takes over from the one looking after Mum. She's not met us before: "She gives thumbs up" she says, encouragingly. At first I don't understand what she's saying. Mum looks comatose. But then she shows us:

"Karen, are you OK? Give me a thumbs up!" she commands. She sounds as if she's talking to someone very old or very deaf. But Mum gives her a thumbs up!

"Can she actually hear us?" I ask.

"Try it… yes! Just speak slowly…".

Dad makes his way over to Mum's right side, where I'm sitting. I'm holding Mum's hand and he asks me to stroke her hand. There are different coloured cannulas in her hand. They jangle a little, like bangles. There's a blue sleeve around her hand and angry red blotches on much of the arm.

"Karen… Tashi is holding your hand… Thumbs up if you can feel it" the nurse says. Mum squeezes my hand. Weakly, but it's there. I stroke the top of her hand. Then she gives a clear thumbs up. It seems unreal to me. What does this mean? Can she hear everything we say? Is she just unable to speak or open her eyes? Dad tries something different. He brings Léa over to Mum's right hand and places Mum's hand on top of her hair. The hand rests on her head for a little bit and then slowly drops away. He brings it up again – a finger moves. Maybe Mum just gives thumbs ups whenever asked to do so.

When we leave Mum, it's very late, again. We're just getting into the car when Dad gets a call he's been waiting for. It's the neurosurgeon and someone Mum actually worked with on a project. The car starts fogging up and I feel a bit sick. It seems endless. I hear the neurosurgeon say things like: "We don't know if her state is due to the stroke or due to the shock… swelling… the brain area where the bleed occurred is irreparably damaged… It's mostly a thalamic stroke, basal ganglia, insula…". The words that stick in my head are "shock" whatever that means, and "irreparable".

It's three days after the stroke. Dad asks Mum some questions to see whether she can answer back.

He's tried this before and there was nothing. But Mum makes more sounds today, so he tries again:

"Can you say Tashi?"
 "Tashi"
 "Can you say Somba?"
 "Somba"
 "That's good…"

We can just about make out Mum's words, but she has a full score. It's wonderful to hear her voice, but her eyes stay shut. It's like talking to someone who is very drowsy. Dad sounds goofy – like he's talking to a pet or small child. He apologises to Mum for sounding like this and I think she's OK with it for now.

Unexpectedly, Mum is moved to a new ward – A3 – and we're disoriented by this. Dad is worried that the move is too quick. We're supposed to take this as a good sign and one of the nurses explained that it's just one step away from critical care. It's confusing, because Mum's not able to say anything like the day before. Something about fighting an infection or something. Although she's off the venti-lator, she wears an oxygen mask and keeps fussing with it, so I try to keep her right hand busy. I Hi-Five Mum and she Hi-Fives back. She seems asleep and her head is away from me. I say "Thumbs up" – she gives a thumbs up. I don't think I ever saw Mum Hi-Five or give a thumbs up to anyone. But when she folds her arm around my little sister, who leans dangerously up against her, it's her alright; you can tell that it's her just by the way she moves her hand.

A thought occurs to me: Why does she not move her left arm at all? It's a thread I don't want to pull on too much. The nurses seem to have just explained it away as something caused by the stroke. But it worries me.

We brought in a scarf for Mum. I chose the blue one she was wearing the previous week – one of her favourites. Léa sniffs it eagerly: "It has Mom's Mummy smell!" she squeals. Today's nurse is relaxed and friendly – she mentions that she has a daughter about the same age as my little sister. After checking with the nurse, Dad lets my sister cuddle with Mum on the bed and Mum holds her gently.

In turn, my sister holds a gangly pink flamingo with peace signs on its bum. A friend had left it in a little silver bag for her. I wonder how she knew that Léa was eyeing this bird every time we walked past the gift shop. That gift shop had been like a magnet to her ever since she came into the hospital. And it is one of those places where we forget, for a moment, about everything other than silly stuffed toys.

The nurse tells us that it's the "best" she's seen Mum all day, pointing to the monitor with its multi-coloured lines. Dad comments that both my sister and I were on similar monitors when we were little. I was almost two months premature: "Yes, your alarm kept going off because you'd stop breathing from time to time…". I wonder how that must have been for Mum and Dad – coming into the hospital for almost two months to look at me – and monitors.

When we get home, my godmother comes over for dinner. She's a neuropsychologist but she and my dad don't talk shop. Instead, there's red wine and chocolates and it feels almost like one of our many game nights. But Mum's not here and there's no point even suggesting playing Ligretto or Uno because Dad admits he's hopeless at it and without Mum it would be no fun.

Sometimes, when we get to the hospital, the visitors' room is already full. It's really a waiting room and the main thing people seem to mark their progress by is whether or not their relative has woken up or opened their eyes. I wonder what happens after that. I browse through all sorts of pamphlets there, trying not to look at the other people, especially when they cry or hug each other. Bits of everyday life also break through on the phone calls – childcare arrangements, feeding the cat. But mostly, the discussions you try not to hear, because they seem too public, but you can't miss them, even with earplugs stuffed in as deep as you can: "He'll get through it…"; "They found his car on the A10"; "Broke some ribs as well… the least of our worries". I can't imagine listening to this conversation anywhere else. In the silences, it just seems as if we're all in the same boat – a very small life raft kind of a boat. With tea, hot chocolate and coffee.

It's sometimes harder when we get updates or compare progress. My dad talks to the other people. Maybe he's being the psychologist to them – gives him something else to think about. There's a Sikh family who basically invite my dad to come to their gurdwara when this is all over. They bring something warm into the waiting room – not just tea and biscuits anymore, but foil wrapped parcels that make me feel so hungry. They must have spotted me looking over and I am delighted when they offer us some home-made samosas in a foil package. I feel like a scavenger, but a satisfied one.

There's a mum whose son is in intensive care again. She talks a lot and shows people photos of him on her phone. Most of the time. "Oh, he's been in here – well – at least three times before…". She sounds like a tourist who keeps visiting the same place. I understand that her son has epilepsy and that he has episodes which require a short stay in ICU. How is that even possible? She's calling his school now and telling them that he's not going to go to school today. Some people in the kitchen never talk about anything medical – they could be anywhere, talking about Facebook posts, recipes, problems at work. It can be even harder listening to them. How does life go on like this for them?

I hide behind some pamphlets – drawings of the brain, Stroke Association. I try not to look at any of the notices, which seem grim. The people on the pamphlet are smiling – they seem delighted as they walk through hospital corridors with their grandma in a wheelchair. It seems unreal to me. There's a pamphlet for my sister as well, and oddly, this seems a bit more to the point as it deals with a mum who no longer talks, walks or smiles. Léa quickly gives up colouring it. I drop my pamphlet as well – maybe it will help someone else.

My dad is on his phone a lot more than I've ever seen him. Normally he just doesn't do social media – that was always Mum's thing. He's letting people know on WhatsApp what's going on. I feel he's telling them more than he tells me. I wonder how he is feeling, I put my hand on his shoulder, but he doesn't look up. Before all this, he would tell me not to be on my phone so much. This seems different and he tells me that Mum is really the social one and that she would want him to be reaching out to people like this.

Even after the kiddy pamphlet, my sister asks: "Did Mummy have a baby?". It is impossible not to laugh a little while I can feel my eyes burning at the same time. She holds some raggedy donated doll with a dangling eyeball. After all the tubes and pamphlets, how can she still be thinking Mum's having a baby? While Dad's busy being CNN with his updates, I take over: "Mummy is ill, she had a stroke – remember?". She still looks confused, I continue "A stroke is when a vein in your brain pops, it's like a bruise inside Mummy's head. Like a balloon". This satisfies her for now, especially the balloon part, but I know there's going to be more. I regret choosing the word "pop", but that's how Mum described her stroke.

I start thinking about school as she slips back into playing with some toys that have had better days. We must remember to donate some of her old toys. I have so much to do for school; aren't the exams ahead? If I don't do well on these, I won't even be able to get into a good sixth form. Jesus, I'll end up going somewhere terrible without any of my friends if I don't get a grip.

What does that even mean? What would I even tell my friends, the teachers? Maybe I should just take all of these pamphlets and shove it at them since I can barely hold on to whatever they're trying to make me understand about stroke.

I'm telling Mum about yesterday. We went to a Hallowe'en themed party that was held in a rambling country house – one of my sister's school friends. I tell her about incredible food and the fun we had. I don't tell her that the party, even if it really was for younger kids, actually helped me to forget about the hospital for a moment. I ended up sitting in between the grown-ups and the kids – something like a teen-age au pair or something. I tell Mum about the rabbit mask Dad wore – something left over from a previous easter party. He looked kind of cute and terrifying at the same time – something between Donny Darko and a rabbit in the headlights.

It was World Stroke Day a day or so ago. My little sister has gone back to school, but I'm allowed to stay at home and "prepare" for my mock exams next week. I have no idea what to do and mostly just sleep or stare at my work. I spend my time mostly avoiding thinking or doing, while Dad seems to be doing the exact opposite.

Dad plays Mum a message from a friend in Hawaii. As he does this, Mum holds up her little finger and thumb in a kind of "Hang loose" surfer-dude sign. There's no other sign that she can hear us other than that right hand. It's the first time she has "said" any-thing other than thumbs up. A nurse tells us she recognised the gesture as a "Shaka", a Hawaiian greeting. This is something much more specific than giving a thumbs up and I am surprised that Mum even knew about this greeting. But Mum's not doing well at all. She's less responsive mostly and has a bad cough.

Mum writes something in the air. I suggest to Dad that he gets her to write on his iPad with her finger and he holds it under her fingertip, which scrawls something on the screen. It could be anything, but I think I can make out "Love" or "Leave" or a reindeer (Christmas is – after all – not too far away). Later, Dad shows me a text from a friend of his which spent some time deciphering the message to mean: "Loveuall", complete with a numbered chart deciphering each of the letters. I wonder whether it is really just a reindeer after all. In all this, it's like we keep looking for Mum and seeing her through little gestures and "signs", which may not mean anything other than that we keep trying to look for her.

It's Hallowe'en and it is freezing. I made a half-hearted attempt at wearing a biker's jacket with bunny ears and my sister insisted on wearing the Cheetah onesie Mum made for her a little while back. Actually, Mum just finished the "Cheetah suit" a day or two ago. Somewhere in my head, there's a list of "last things Mum did". Léa insists on wearing the onesie, even though I try hopelessly to convince her that it's too cold. We compromise and I am allowed to wrap her in some tiger skin material. I go for leather jacket and bunny ears. We look an odd pair as Dad

drives us through some more promising neighbour-
hoods looking for lit pumpkins and treats. He doesn't
have to say it, but I know that this is for Mum because
she always loved Hallowe'en. Everything we do outside
the hospital feels a bit like this – going through the
motions of stuff even if we don't want to. Maybe my
dad is trying to prove to himself and others that we
somehow still function.

When we get back to the hospital, we do our best
to share Hallowe'en with Mum, but she's not doing
at all well. They tell us that she has physiotherapy to
help with her chest. Dad's convinced that she is
struggling now because they allowed her to choke on
her own vomit when she was first admitted. A nurse
strikes up a conversation with me and asks me how
old my sister is. She tells me that she has a daughter
the same age. She looks at my little sister, again
wearing the Cheetah onesie, cuddling with Mum. The
nurse tears up and rushes from the room. It is not
going well for my sister, who has had some "acci-
dents" at school, after which some boys have been
teasing her. I can hardly bear going to school myself.

I feel as if I can just keep slipping through the
cracks – then no one would take notice and I would
not have to try to explain anything to anyone, myself
included. It is weekend and Dad takes Léa to all the
things he lined up for her. Mercifully I don't have to
tag along. He takes her to Alliance Française, to
gymnastics and then to an indoor gym meeting
organised by friends. I lie on my bed, listening to
music and hugging my dog. Now and then I look at

the buzzing phone on my side table. Now and then I respond to a text or a friend I can no longer ignore. It feels good not to be in public, at the hospital. But I feel guilty for just enjoying being in my own room instead of feeling the need to be with Mum or my family today.

Dad gets a call from a nurse and he's immediately expecting the worst. As we go to the hospital, I automatically start taking my sister to the ward we last saw Mum in, but Dad catches up with us and takes us to NCCU again. It's the weirdest feeling to be back there: Almost as if we're home again, and my sister seems delighted because she's back in the friendlier kitchen with its run-down toys and squash. Dad also seems more relaxed here, because the previous ward just did not seem to be intensive enough for Mum. I can sense that he's angry and irritated too, thinking that the move to the less intensive ward was a bad choice which has now led to a setback. We find out from an actual doctor, rarer than unicorns, that they attempted an "EVD Challenge" ("Extra Ventricular Drain" – removing the drain in Mum's brain). Why would you try to "challenge" someone in Mum's state? The doctor thought that the "challenge" led to a "drop in functioning". Can Mum afford a further "drop in functioning"? We seem to have so little of Mum – one "responsive" right hand and now this.

Dad was very angry about the "EVD challenge" and tells me about something that happened when I was still in the NICU. I sometimes stopped breathing, as many premature babies do, and instead of giving me oxygen, one nurse made a point of taking me from Mum and refusing to give me oxygen so that I could "learn to breathe". I got bluer and bluer and did not breathe – stubborn from the start. In the end, the nurse reluctantly put the oxygen mask back onto me. A day or two later she apologised for being so pushy.

It's two days after the EVD challenge and today Mum opens her eyes and is back in the thumbs up and hand squeezing business! But her face is still expressionless. There's no smile when we come in. Just a fixed stare. Now and then I make out other emotions in her eyes – or at least I think I do. She looks in turns bewildered, frightened or sad. I say nothing of what I see out loud but can only imagine how confusing and terrifying this must be to her. I can't explain it properly, but the image of the little robin we see whenever we go den building in the park comes to mind. Mum is just like that little robin, hiding in the bushes. Now and then he suddenly appears, but mostly you don't see him at all. But when you do catch a glimpse, it makes up for everything.

Mum suddenly got much sicker and less responsive again. I don't feel the same degree of panic anymore, perhaps because the nurses in NCCU seem so matter of fact about things. But on the plus side, she ended up in her own side-room because of an infection. This is the first time, after A&E, that I actually get to be with Mum in something like privacy and it feels incredible. It's as if I couldn't really just focus on being with her when there's someone else's mum or son in the next bed. Some of the nurses are just incredible (I like the ones with "personality", who actually relate to us). One nurse with an American accent actually makes notes of what my sister was reading in my Mum's diary, "So that your mom's not left out, you know!". I wonder whether Mum would ever have the chance to read these notes, but it seems such a kind thing to do.

My sister and I have just had our eyes tested. On top of everything else, I need glasses. There's a knot in my stomach as Dad drags me from optician to optician. He keeps handing me frame after frame and I like each new frame less and less. He has something to say about the few frames I like and I'm not too bothered anyway, since I probably won't actually wear the glasses much. We rush back to the hospital, frameless for now. If Mum was with me, I'm sure she would have found a way to agree with something I chose. We tell Mum about the opticians, unsure what she takes in. Dad plays her some recordings made by friends in China, Egypt… she squeezes his hand, opens her eyes and gives thumbs up in response. I hold her hand and ask whether she would like to arm wrestle with me. She squeezes my hand and we actually arm wrestle! I'm surprised at the strength I feel in her arm.

When we get home, we're absolutely exhausted. I'm sitting at the dinner table with Léa when Dad suddenly starts laughing out loud. The dog is looking quizzically at him, and Dad explains: "Oh my goodness, I'm so tired. I almost gave him a dishwasher tablet instead of his pills!". I know just how he feels.

Mum is now in her own side bed because her stomach has been upset. They're taking no chances.

They don't know whether she caught a stomach bug or whether it's just a side effect of the high dose of antibiotics she takes. Well, if that's what it takes to get a bit of privacy! They also don't know why she has a high temperature, which could be because of an infection or because of her stroke, which could lead to fatal hyperthermia. Mum is surrounded by fans in their attempt to bring her temperature down. We wait for a doctor to give us an update since the nurses are not allowed to do this. After more than an hour and a half of further waiting and being told the doctor is just about to come, Dad gets really naughty and leads us in signing: "Ms Polly had a dolly who was sick, sick, sick, she called for the doctor and...". Laughing, we take turns to change the words to things like: "But he said he couldn't come quick, quick, quick". We go home without seeing the doctor, because it is way beyond my sister's bedtime.

Why should this account matter? I look back at what I've written so far and at what I've read and have to remind myself again: It does. It simply does. My dad introduced me to the Survivors' Stories series of books published by Routledge, of people with brain injury. I've dipped into them, but when I asked my dad whether anyone has ever written about the experience of a family or specifically a teenager, there was nothing. In fact, I would later learn, there has been fairly limited research on teenagers' experience of their parents' illness or specifically their acquired brain injury or stroke.

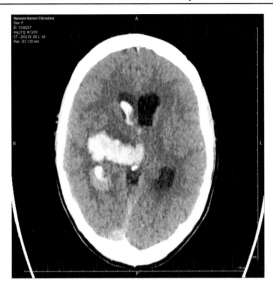

Figure 1.1. CT-scan of brain taken on the day of the stroke

So, a part of me is writing this for you – if you're out there and made time to read this after putting down Instagram, Snapchat or whatever. I'm writing this for myself too. I wish that I had read something – anything – written by someone like me at some point following my mum's stroke. Something other than a pamphlet. If you're anything like me, you will be feeling quite alone and perhaps even more abnormal than you already feel as a teenager. I will not presume I know you, but perhaps there are some things for you in this account of what my mother, my family and I have been through.

I have always loved poetry and remember the first poem I ever memorised – Blake's "The Tyger" – as a child. At some point, my dad shared Elizabeth

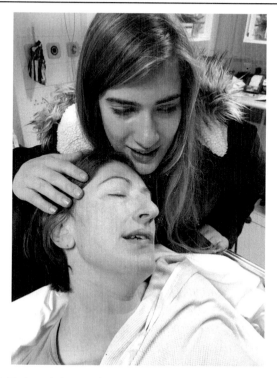

Figure 1.2. Tashi with her mother in A&E on admission for suspected stroke

Bishop's poem "One Art" with me. Read it. The lines: "…so many things seem filled with the intent to be lost…" struck me. It felt to me like I was one of those things after Mum's stroke. Not only did I feel lost, I wanted to be lost as well. Of course, the poem is really ironic: It is extremely hard to lose someone, or even just to lose what you believed or expected about them, or yourself.

The first thing to know is that they say that there are these stages of grief or loss and that you may feel it.

Classically, Elizabeth Kübler Ross wrote about the stages of grief in her 1969 book On Death and Dying. *She built this theory on her work with terminally ill patients and identified a series of five distinct emotional phases in people who experience grief: Denial, anger, bargaining, depression and acceptance. As with all things scientific, this model has been criticised over the years and Kübler Ross wrote about how people do not in fact go through these stages of grief in a "linear and predictable" way. I sure didn't; none of my family did. Anyway, my mum is not dead.*

So, there are models and more models and this is not a science or psychology class. But it is important to know that if your parent had a stroke or brain injury, you will be experiencing many of these stages at different times. To me these stages were more like being stuck on a rollercoaster that's just going so fast that you're just feeling sick or scared most of the time. Even if other people are on the same rollercoaster as you, they're too busy clinging on themselves to help you much.

Some sources of stress you will experience relate to: Seeing your parent injured, experiencing the hospitalisation of your parent and being really scared that your parent could die. Then there's the slow unfolding difficulties relating to the impairments your mum or dad would have. Some are more obvious than others: Physical difficulties, problems with their thinking (cognitive difficulties), and other difficulties relating to their social and emotional functioning. There's also the stress of your healthy parent's reaction to the whole situation.

All these factors were present for me. But there's more: The literature also talks about "secondary" stresses: Disruptions to parenting, changes in relationships, shifts in perspectives on the future, stress about finances and hardship, social stigmatisation.

I think the first step in dealing with the crisis of what happened to us is to know that this is stressful and that you're not bad for finding this difficult. It is difficult and will continue to be difficult for you and your family for a very long time.

I think it is very important to find something that you can do in the crisis stage. We kept getting these little food parcels from people and it was great to have something easy and home cooked; maybe to play a board game or something afterwards. Maybe it would have helped me if we had some more predictable rituals and things to do. Maybe I could have cooked a meal a week or something. It is so important to feel that you are doing something useful and constructive, even if it feels nothing else you do has any point to it.

One of our family rituals was to go on walks with our dog into a nearby park. He loved it and we became friends with a robin who kept on appearing, as if it knew about us. We also tried some den building. And of course, the trips to the hospital with all the little stops along the way become some sort of "new normal", but then it changes. Especially in the early days. There's really no predictability and my mum kept moving between different hospital beds, wards and procedures. That was really hard, as hospitals seem to run on processes like this and just as soon as you've built up some sense of comfort in a shabby waiting room or a friendly nurse, you have to move on to another ward, where it may feel your parent doesn't belong.

Then there's the sense of unreality – call it denial if you like. For me, it kept feeling so unreal. There was something about seeing that smokestack of the hospital in the distance and knowing that's where Mum is, that made things more real. But my advice – if I can give any – is to prepare for different shades of dissociating or cutting off from the reality that you and your family are facing. Don't be too freaked out about this. No one says you have to feel anything…. Maybe it will take you time. Sometimes, it's the worst thing to feel that there's something wrong with you for not feeling more, or for not really treating the whole disaster that has hit your family as you think you should be treating it. I just cut off and spaced out much of those early days. Exhaustion can take many forms and our family sometimes just seemed to run on fumes. You also don't really fully recharge your energy by sleep or anything else that previously helped.

Then there's the unexpected – every moment of it. Especially at first. We were absolutely amazed at never having any part of the process explained to us. Evidently some hospitals have case workers who can be in touch and who can walk you through what to expect at different stages: I think ours was on some kind of permanent sick leave or something. Dad kept trying to be in touch with her. It made little difference that my dad actually is a clinical psychologist working *in brain injury: We were just as lost in those corridors. And we were just as stuck in front of those buzzers and ward doors that did not open. Often, the only solution we found was to complain to PALS (Patient Advice and Liaison Service). Some staff would actually tell us to contact them. But each time, this was a whole trauma as well for us, as you feel you don't want to make a fuss or take anyone's attention off actually caring for patients. Mostly it just seemed that a little bit of information goes a long way and that the hospital ends up wasting its own time by eventually having to go the PALS route instead of just keeping people informed.*

Chapter 2

We're in this together

I can hear my sister humming to herself as we walk down the hospital corridors. It's like we live here. Every time we visit, Léa is attracted to the gift shop, which has surprisingly nice things – at least in her opinion. Some multi-coloured *worry monsters* are hanging against the far wall and she's really attracted to these because she heard about them at school. "Can I have one?" she asks. My dad looks at the price tag – of course he knows he should just buy her one, but every time he doesn't. We're going to be here for a while and he keeps any such treats in reserve, for when we really need them. I stick my fist into the throat of the worry monster. "Choke on this" I think. Nothing can take my worries away at this point.

We're on autopilot as a family. It feels bizarre to visit someone who doesn't know you're visiting. Or maybe she does? I am so torn with every visit as I feel so tired. My dad does his best to add variety to the visits – not that it helps me much, but it seems to work sometimes. He makes a point of showing us some of the art against the walls. It seems like a really big effort for

DOI: 10.4324/9781003171676-2

him, but normally whenever we go anywhere, Dad would try taking us to an art gallery and I guess he's making do here. My sister is entranced by "the one with all the colourful animals", which invites everyone to "find your oasis". Wouldn't that be nice? I think to myself. Not here, that's for sure.

We are stunned when we get to Mum's bed and she's not there. A much older woman with some staples in her head is lying there. It feels like my stomach drops out. I mean, I know people are busy, but maybe they should have a map or something or give you a quick update when you come into the ward. Where is she? A nurse turns to us: "She was moved upstairs", she says as she turns back to her patient. Is this good news? Bad news? We've been moving between wards with only different numbers to distinguish themselves – A2, A3, A4. We are becoming so disoriented that we sometimes walk automatically to the previous ward Mum was in, instead of going to the current one.

It's almost like moving home or going to a new school – we got so used to the previous ward; the waiting room, the sounds. We find our way to the new ward, but it takes forever since we make some wrong turns. My sister looks bewildered. It is such a different ward: Fewer nurses, not as many machines, less of everything. We walk past some of the rooms on the ward – men and women separate. I can see patients on their mobile phones, tapping out messages. Surely, this can't be right – they all seem so much more aware than Mum. When we get to Mum, the ventilator has been taken out; her eyes are open. My little sister is overenthusiastic: "Mummy! You're awake!".

Mum makes no reply and her eyes seem vacant, even frightened. But I make out just a twitch of a smile. "Hi, I'm the nurse in charge of the ward today, Karen was moved here last night. Her condition has stabilized since we fitted the shunt."

"Shunt?" I ask. "Yes, it's essentially a valve which we can control to reduce the amount of pressure in her brain" he pauses, indicating the shaved patch on her head from which a tube protrudes. The tube is disconcerting. We learn that it's a drain to relieve pressure. It's not as if I hadn't seen Mum inject herself with insulin; she even wore an insulin pump. But she was always very discrete about it. It was there, but also not there. Her bald skull, the tube… this is very much there. My sister seems to recoil at the bald head and the tube. Even the word "drain" is worrying. What's it draining?

We sit by the bed, holding Mum's hand. Some kindly nurse had put on daytime telly for Mum and it seems just wrong. She'd never sit through a *Jeremy Kyle* episode, instead listening to audiobooks or doing sudoku if she had nothing better to do. Mum doesn't respond and her eyes are closed most of the time. We tell her that we're there and what's going on, but she doesn't give any indication of response.

"I love you Mum" I say, if she can understand me, I want her to know this and to hold on to this. I think back to that book that we read when I was little: *The*

Kissing Hand. But this time, I'm doing the mummy raccoon's job instead of the other way around. I kiss Mum's hand and tell her that the kiss will stay there as long as she needs it. I feel her squeeze my hand in response. I look for a smile, but it's not there yet.

Dad keeps trying to cope by being action man. He's trying to organise audiobooks for Mum, as he thinks it's her thing and that she would be stimulated by it. But the trouble is actually getting the nurses to find time to assist with this. Imagine being plugged into an audiobook you don't like for 20 hours on end. Or listening to the same chapter over and over again because someone had accidently placed it on loop or something. But then again, that's exactly how I feel at the moment.

I try to do some schoolwork; I dread going back to school next Monday but I guess it has to happen sometime and maybe it will take my mind off things. It's so hard to concentrate in here, distracted by other patients, nurses talking loudly, food trollies and ward routines. I sigh, it's no use. So, we sit by the bed and wait. My dad reads to my little sister. I am jealous: I want something to do that feels like it matters. It's so hard just sitting like this. My mind keeps going back to that painting we saw on our way in: Where is my oasis?

I think that before all this, I'd have said it was our home but now it's just a reminder of everything that's changed. I remember when I was younger the garden was my oasis. I could spend hours, even in a small backyard, looking at birds, being in nature, being a part of nature. Here, we seem very far away from nature. At first, I thought we should be bringing in flowers, cards… but that's not allowed when people are this ill. So, it looks nothing like the unrealistic hospital rooms of the many American shows I've seen. The beds are crammed in so close that it's hard not to feel as if you're intruding on another family whenever they visit. And it's so clinical and functional. Maybe when she gets better, we'll be allowed to bring in things to cheer her up.

After what seems hours, my dad turns to me "Are you hungry?". I look at the time – already 5pm. We haven't even eaten lunch, I'm not hungry but I know I should probably eat anyway. I've lost my appetite recently but eating feels like something that marks the day; something that we can at least do and that has a real purpose. Something I can accomplish.

It takes ages to say goodbye to Mum and to scrape up all our stuff. Dad is touchy about all our stuff lying on floors, chairs, etc. It seems important not to get in the way of the staff. There is no indication that Mum has heard our many goodbyes. It feels like life slowly returns as we make our way to the food court. Here things feel more normal, almost as if we're having a family day out or something and just taking a quick break in some museum cafeteria. Today, there are pop-up shops in the concourse and my sister squeals with delight at some little wooden fairies and goblins before we drag her off, protesting a little. I helped Mum put up a little fairy door in Léa's room and she keeps putting things in front of it – flecks of oats, a tiny piece of apple – so that she can coax the fairies out. We end up just getting coffee and hot chocolate since it's far too busy today to have a meal.

We get into the car, "What's for dinner?" I ask, not particularly caring but my little sister should eat anyway.

He shrugs but asks Léa what she would like.

She frowns and ponders a second, "We're going to McDonalds!" She announces, proud of this brilliant idea. I wrinkle my nose, "I don't know…". I look at my dad, but he just looks exhausted: "I'll re-heat some leftovers – we can just have a verskeidenheid". A verskeidenheid is Afrikaans for a mini-buffet on a plate; a mix of food.

We sit around the table. It is too strange, eating without Mum. She always enjoyed whatever Dad made. It took me a while to set the table, as the three settings looked wrong, but my mind just could not work it out: I kept wanting to set another place for Mum. But there's something normal and comforting in having food at home and I eat despite my lack of hunger: Maybe we'll get through this.

When we finish dinner, I take the dog for a walk. It's late and not the best weather, but this is the best moment of my day. For me, it feels like the only time of the day when I am actually free. I know I should be getting home, but I can spend the night on the bench, watching my dog running around in the park. The lamps are beginning to shine their buttery-yellow lights, only just. There is so much joy in the dog as he runs after birds – no chance he would ever really catch them, but he doesn't give up. He's so fluffy and most people laugh when they see him, because he just looks so goofy. I think Mum was really his favourite, because she always gave him food. Does he know she's not with us? Maybe he can smell her still after our visits, although I doubt it. He looks at me ser-iously – I convince myself he's just concerned about food. We probably smell of hospital and hospital food by now, not that he'd mind.

"Hey there good boy," I say, stroking his soft fur fondly, "has anyone told you what's going on?". He looks up at me – for a ridiculous second I think maybe he understands me, or maybe he just feels my sadness, but then a trespassing squirrel catches his attention and he bounds off, barking joyfully. By the time it's getting dark, there's still a faint pink streak in the sky. I love sunsets. But in the distance, I see the blinking light and the darker outline of the incin-erator at the hospital. Time to go home. On the notice board by my bed is a scribbled note: "School tomorrow!". I had completely forgotten. Maybe it will be good to get back to "normal"… I doubt it.

I wake early, before sunrise. I can't move. I lie in bed wondering whether this is how Mum feels. I just can't move. I don't want to. But how would it be if I really couldn't will myself into action? Is this how the stroke felt? I think of her as I drag myself out of bed. It seems lazy and silly of me to make such a show of getting up. But – yes – I feel sorry for myself. Why did this have to happen? It feels strange to put on my uniform even though it had only been two weeks. I feel too old for the uniform. It feels like a costume or something I may have worn to Comicon – dress up. Do people even take school seriously anymore? I mean – Jesus – I almost saw my mum die. And I helped her not to choke on her own vomit. Should I say that when other people tell me about their holiday? I imagine their conversations:

> We went camping… again… such a drag. It was so cold…
>
> My little sister wanted to go to the Harry Potter thing – it sucked – nothing like the films really. Just trying to sell you fake butter beer.
>
> Well, I just got to stay home – nothing much happening – just watching television.

It's wrong of me to think this, but I imagine myself shouting or something. Just to stop all the normal, all the whinging. Maybe I will say something like:

Well, I got to see the inside of a hospital. I saw a lot of nurses; fewer doctors. I saw a lot of car parks. And I saw my mum. I stayed with her – just waiting for her to say something – anything! Sometimes we think she may even have scribbled or said something. Even having a go at me for my room being a mess would have been good. She's had a stroke and that's that… maybe she'll get better, maybe not. What the fuck… count yourself lucky if you just got to sit in front of Netflix all the time. I didn't even get to do that.

That would be one hell of a way of keeping friends, I'm sure.

"Why aren't you ready for school?" my dad seems angry. It's like he's expecting me to have my shit together. Normally my mother would be filling in the gaps – everything would be so much smoother. Now, we've got to do it all. He's tried for almost a quarter of an hour and he's made a bit of a mess of my sister's hair, but at least he's trying. Can't blame him for not having long hair himself to practice on. I shake myself into action, like our dog, shaking off a cuddle.

We have so little time: First we've got to drop Léa off at breakfast club as soon as we possibly can and then we're rushing against the traffic to school. Normally she'd hardly be awake by now. We have no family here – no friends to plug the gaps really. Not that my dad moans too much about it – not that there's time for moaning. It seems impossible to ask for help and when he does, there's always some vague offer that never comes to anything. Too many: "We really should…" empty offers and playdates that don't really materialise. We're on our own – more or less – in this.

The drive to school is half-an-hour long – on a good day. Before my mum's stroke, things would be easier, and silence would have seemed easier – like something we could fill if we wanted to. Now the silences sit between us like a huge ugly soap bubble about to burst. None of the easy chatter of before. We talk about logistics: "You're going to have to get the train home today – OK?". I think, underneath it, we're just both so tired.

"Yeah that's fine" I say, trying not to sound too reluctant but I'm already so tired. We all are, and I am afraid of telling my dad just how tired I feel. He's tired too. Join the club. I don't even know if he sleeps much. Hell – I don't even know if I sleep much. "I've emailed the school already, so they know that Mum…" he pauses "well, they know everything, so don't worry". That sounds stupid, coming from him. He worries about everything. I suppose he has to. But in this case, I'm not worried. Maybe I should be – I haven't done an ounce of schoolwork and I've not been for a week so. Who knows how much I've missed already? It all just feels so pointless.

I get out of the car and watch my dad drive off. I feel awful and lost – a little like my little sister today, who quickly hid her fear with a hug as we left her at breakfast club. I wish I could just run after the car and yell: "I'm not ready yet!". Maybe I can tell him I'm ill or something – I have a headache most of the time anyway, so it won't be untrue. Maybe I inherited whatever was wrong with Mum. My head pounds. *Hypochondriac*. I say to myself. Of course, there's nothing wrong with my head – not really. Not like Mum. I feel like it's my first day at school as I look at my timetable. A disaster – too much to take in. But at least it's real: "English". My first class, saying it out loud makes me feel a little reassured. But then I check my phone – I'm late. Very.

I don't know how I get there; as I walk into the classroom, I can feel that everyone's looking at me, my skin prickles. I take my seat and unpack my things – I hear a whisper next to me, "Hey, you disappeared. You OK?" It's the girl I sit next to, what was her name – Annabel? Ashley? Something like that. "Oh yeah, just family stuff," I shrug "nothing much" she nods and loses interest.

"Right, we're reading *Lord of the Flies* right now – it's really bad" she grimaces "just about some kids who…" the teacher interrupts: "No whispering in my classroom – is there something you'd like to share?" We both shake our heads, certainly not. She turns a bright shade of crimson: "No, sir. Sorry sir". Ah, what a joy it is to be back.

As I'm leaving the room, I hear my name, it's my teacher.

"Tashi, I just want you to know that I understand your situation is difficult right now and if at any point you need some time out in lessons or someone to talk to…" he trails off. You don't really want to be saying that, do you? I think to myself.

I hate being treated differently. Makes me stand out. More than this – I hate looking vulnerable, especially at school. Although I've never been bullied as much as I could have been, I learned early on that it's better to shrug things off. I fear that any vulnerability will cling to me like a bad smell. Despite all the rhetoric and assemblies, that's just how it is. You don't want to become "one of them"; like the kids who frequently take refuge in the "Hub". Once you're one of "them" that's it – no more normality. I want to cling to whatever normality I can.

I guess it's thoughtful of the teacher, but still. It's not like he actually cares or anything. I smile anyway and thank him, "have a good day, sir." He seems relieved, "You too, and send my best wishes to your mum". I knew I wasn't going to but for the sake of common politeness I nodded. She would not know him anyway.

I walk to where I know my friends will be, I hope they're not angry at me for being so off grid – I've barely talked to them in the last week. As I approach one of my best friends, she sees me. "Tashi!" she exclaims excitedly, then her face changes as if she's checking herself – maybe feeling guilty for seeming too excited or happy. Before I know it, I'm surrounded, being hugged by all of my friends as they all speak at once, asking so many questions. Luckily, they don't give me much time to answer. It feels almost as if they practiced this, agreeing before not to make me feel as if I really have to tell them anything. But then they suddenly fall silent, all looking expectantly, waiting for me to speak. I have never felt so awkward with people I'm so close to: "Yeah so… my mum had a stroke." It's my tough voice – like everyone in high school, I've practiced this for long enough to be able to draw on it when I need to. Like I'm saying: "Well, shit happens" or something. Almost like talking about a test I failed or something. My eyes burn and my throat feels tight.

More questions. All about how I am, how my family is, is my mum OK? I barely have an answer to any of these questions. Of course, I'm not OK and they know this. No one in my immediate family is OK just now. It feels like I can't even imagine what OK would be in this situation. I make my best effort to keep appearances up, but a part of me wishes for something other than this. Can't we just change the subject perhaps? I wish I could just tell them: "I don't know how I feel..." instead of trying to figure out how I do feel.

Normally, I'm the one who is there for my friends. They don't know about this, but a year or so ago I went to the GP with my dad after I had headaches for a while. It was a kind doctor about the age of my mum who listened to my story and, after a while, she figured it out: I'm the one always taking care of everyone else. At least when it came to my friends. And, yes, maybe also my mum. She has diabetes and I have learned to get the Ribena whenever it looks like she's got a hypo. The doctor told me at the time that she was just like me and that I must remember to look after myself as well, otherwise I will just keep holding all this tension and worry for other people inside of me. At the time I nodded, but of course little changed. That's my job. I'm the one supposed to be there for my friends, not the other way around and I feel almost as if I can jump out of my own skin with all this care and attention coming at me now.

It is actually a relief when the bell rings and we have to trudge back to class. At least there I don't have to feel too much or talk to people too much. The day passes quickly. I get a few more weird glances from teachers – one or two even seem a little tearful. I feel a bit like I'm at a funeral or something and I break off eye contact quicker than normal. No friendly joking around with the teachers today I'm afraid. I miss that; I miss normal, as messed up as normal used to be.

There's the usual chaos in the corridors. There's an endless queue at the canteen. It feels so different from the hospital, where everyone except the doctors and staff has some kind of sad or at least scary story to tell. It is all so average. I love it and don't want it to end. Even the smell of bad food and the crappy conversations about nail polish, boys, girls – whatever. It's all so average really and I want it never to end.

I get the bus home, the seats are cracked and dusty but a welcome kind of comfortable old, I watch the other people on the bus. They all have their own private lives, with X-boxes, Play stations, Instagram, Snapchat, mums, dads and things. Sure, Nanna may be getting old or demented somewhere, but that's normal. It just doesn't feel right that Mum suddenly had a stroke. A part of me feels jealous of these other blissfully unaware travellers on the bus. Lucky them. They should appreciate it while they have it.

Finally, the bus pulls up to the train station, my school is in a tiny Fenland town, so to get home I've got to get the bus, then train, then walk another half hour. Today this all feels great. Like there's something for me to do really. This feels much better than to open the front door and find no one else there. To not find Mum there. The train slowly pulls into the station, it's full of commuters. They seem important. My uniform marks me out as someone who shouldn't really be in any kind of rush at all. They all push to get in or to get out of the train. I stand patiently and wait for all the shoving and settling to stop.

I plug my earphones in – the right one isn't really working, so I feel a bit unbalanced as I surf along in the train. Now and then I make out the words – it's a band I really like – *Cage the Elephant*. It's their song *Social Cues*. Above the clack of the wheels and the noise in the carriage, I hear snatches from the song: "I don't have the strength… Hide me in the back room… I'll be in the back room". That's where I really want to be – the back room, although I have no idea what I'll be doing there or who will eventually come and look for me there. I almost miss my station, where the shoving starts again. I wonder what would actually happen if I just stay on the train. Just stop doing anything. Just stop making any choices and just let myself be taken along.

By the time I reach home I'm exhausted. Not my usual brand of exhausted. The dog isn't even there to greet me when I shut the door behind me. It's only 5 o'clock but instead of feeling any actual emotions, the only thing I feel – really is tired. And beneath that I feel something else, darker. Maybe irritation or anger. I can't be sure. I flop onto my bed, not even bothering to take my shoes off, and lie there for almost an hour. I feel spacey and it makes me think of *Snow Patrol*'s *Chasing Cars* and that's what I do for a while – just lying there.

It's nice to just not think about anything at all, not sleeping, just not doing anything. I know when my dad and sister get home everything will be rushed again. Not just rushed, it will be like all our lives change gear like a wind-up toy which is wound too tightly – we are so coping, aren't we? I hear the washing machine downstairs whine as it gives everything a final spin, then beep. How do I hear this all the way up in my room? I've got to take the washing out, and empty the dishwasher, and take out the bins, and change my sheets and – I stop myself. Maybe make a to do list. That would be something at least. There's too much to do and what's the point really? So, instead, I just lie on my bed.

At some point I must have drifted off because my dad and sister have just come home. Front door shutting. Dad calling. I hear my name two, three times. "I'm not here" I want to call down. Imagine. "Hey Dad" I call down, secretly praying he doesn't ask me to come downstairs. "Tashi, could you come here – we've got to visit Mum now". It's the last thing I want to do. This sounds bad, so I try to not think it, but I imagine just being in my room instead of at the hospital again. All those smells hitting me. I feel nauseous just thinking about it. I try to talk myself into it: It's not like she asked for it! All her other family is in Canada. My dad keeps saying we have to be there to make sure she's well looked after and that she knows we are there with her and for her. But maybe just my dad could go tonight… just tonight. "I'll be right there!" I shout instead and do nothing to get ready.

When he calls sometime later, this time sounding more impatient, I change quickly. He asks me about my day. He's trying to do stuff in the kitchen, but it seems hopeless, and I can see he's annoyed that I obviously had not done much. It looks bad tonight. We should really just stay here and sort things out for a bit. Both of us know this. "Sorry, Dad, I'm really tired I just – I forgot to do the washing…", I lie. There is a part of me that wants to tell my dad how I feel, but how can I? There's not even time to talk now as both of us give cleaning the kitchen a half-hearted go.

He'd never know it, but I feel bad for having done so little. Maybe I just want Mum to come back and do those things that we have all suddenly become aware of. How were all these things done? I try to tell myself that we are all in this together and that I have a place, a role to play in all this. But as the endless days of school and hospital visits go on, I just feel sapped. We're in this together and I don't like where we are.

We fetch my boyfriend at the train station. There's something so normal and so normally embarrassing about the whole thing. Dad seems almost happy. We'd been together for only 6 months and I feel uncomfortable about this trip. He offered to come along with me to see Mum – he had met her many times before. My mouth feels dry. How are we even going to do this? Only two people are allowed to visit at any time and Dad and my sister will have to leave us with Mum and maybe go to the food court or hang around the giftshops. When we get to Mum, she's unresponsive. She's back in NCCU again. After Dad and my sister leave us, my boyfriend talks to Mum as if she can actually hear him. He talks about life at school and his plans (to become a vet). And I feel such relief: It's not at all as awkward as I imagined. I thought we'd just get there and stare at one another, both thinking that this is a really bad idea. "He's really kind to her, and to me…" I find myself thinking and I feel a little guilty about how I've been cutting myself off from everyone. It feels good to actually bring him into this strange world I've been in with my Mum.

Afterwards, we take the bus into town on our own. I've not been into town for such a long time that it's difficult at first to adjust to the crowds who are already starting to shop for Christmas. We eat take-out and window shop. I forget about everything for a while – no hospital or exams – just responding to the stuff around me. I am so reluctant to take the bus back home. Is that bad of me? Selfish?

My grandmother ("Mormor" in Danish) comes to visit from Canada. The visit started all wrong, with her arriving from the plane then bus then train in front of our locked front door. Incredibly, someone who has a child in the same school as my sister saw her at our front door and took her in. We have no idea how the times got muddled or who was early or late. Dad is mortified and all smiles to the woman who had temporarily taken my grandmother into her busy home – little kids, toys everywhere. Later that evening, after all the apologies, and greetings, I hear the silences. Obviously, we need to visit Mum as we always do, but this visit would be different. I wonder what my grandmother expects to find or how she feels, other than being exhausted after the long flight.

We are at the ward. My grandmother is impressed with how we know our way around the place. So far Mum has been in around seven different wards in the little more than three weeks she has been in hospital. It's actually a wonder that they have not misplaced her somewhere. My grandmother and I are at Mum's bed. It is a bit awkward at first, since we were reminded that Mum can only have two visitors at a time. I feel at a loss about where I should be. Someone always has to be with Léa, and my dad volunteers, so they set off for the concourse. I don't want to go with them, I don't want to stay. I feel so uncomfortable seeing my grandmother with Mum for the first time. It feels so wrong. My dad always says that the worst thing imaginable for a parent is to have a sick child or to lose a child. I think back to all those times we were in Canada with my grandmother. Mum is the only daughter, the one supposed to be offering to help out in the kitchen or with the shopping. Seeing my grandmother hold Mum's hand and getting tearful is difficult.

I am so close to "adulthood" whatever that means, but there's a part of me that just doesn't want to believe that adults are fragile and that they can't always take care of their children, let alone themselves. Seeing my grandmother with my mum feels like this. I get a flashback to A&E, that first night of Mum's stroke. One of the last things she said was: "I love my Mummy", like a little child, while also worrying about Léa. This is a tricky thing for me to think: Adults are children; parents are children too who sometimes want nothing more than the comfort of a parent; being a child again for a bit. I wonder what this means for me growing up. Will I be like this too one day when something terrible happens in my life? I can't imagine it. I wonder whether Mum will even wake up or be aware enough of my grandmother before she has to leave again for Canada.

There's a package waiting on the porch for me when we get home. I open it eagerly, since I am expecting some black shoes to replace my worn-out Vans which I need for school. The shoes in the package are tiny. They are black; they are Vans, but I am not even sure that they will fit my little sister! I show them to Dad when he gets home. He's apologetic and explains that he ordered them online and must have not noticed that they're the kids' size 7. It will be another week or so before I get a different pair, because we're simply too busy to go to the shop.

I tell Mum about the shoes when we see her. The nurses have tied her hair into Panda bunches like I sometimes tie my sister's hair. My sister is obviously delighted and wants Mum's hair always to look just like this. Mum manages little nods and shakes of the head now. We still have to watch really closely for any expressions, but she sometimes raises an eyebrow (a question perhaps), frowns a bit and so on. Mum explores her face with her right hand. She feels her hair and tries to touch the left side of her face but doesn't quite manage. Dad holds up his phone in selfie mode so that she can see herself mirrored in it. She stares at it intently, as if she's seeing herself for the first time. I wonder what she makes of those Panda bunches and distract her by telling her about how my sister pretends to meditate like Kung Fu Panda for all of 5 seconds before getting bored.

People who research families' responses to parental ill health write about the process of feeling a sense of unity – us against something. And maybe we did feel a bit more of it. We did feel like a team after the initial shock of what happened to Mum. I think it's so important to feel that you're still part of things in this phase.

For me, it was returning to school. This introduced the business of making a long commute to school and throwing myself – as much as possible – back into things I no longer really cared about. That was really hard for me. How can you care about homework, or about your friends' problems if you feel that you've been through hell with your family? How can you care about other people's losses? But still: Knowing that you're together in this, in this together, makes some kind of difference.

My dad had support from his colleagues, and this spilled over to me. I was overwhelmed by my friends' reaction and support. My personality is to be the caring or supporting one, so it felt really wrong to be on the receiving end of this – from teachers, from friends… but it did and does help to be a bit more open to this and to let it be. Also, to know that we are – all of us – actually in this together. Sometimes someone would come up to me and tell me of their own loss; maybe a grandparent or someone else that was ill. I did feel different from them, because my once fit and

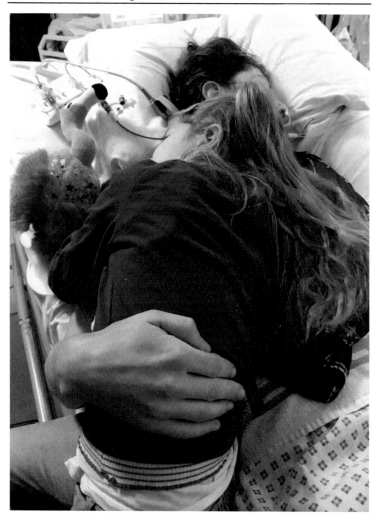

Figure 2.1. Karen hugs Léa while still minimally responsive

active mum who was always so clever and who could do everything all the time was suddenly taken into hospital. I learned not to push these normal things

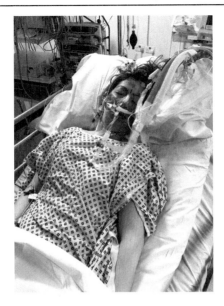

Figure 2.2. Karen in NCCU

away from me early on, although I was probably helped by the front I could put up. I wanted to cry but didn't really. My friends kind of held the emotion for me at the time and – looking back – I think I was probably falling into some degree of depression.

There is such a lot of concern and care available, but it comes at you from so many directions all at once. I just wanted things to be as normal as possible. It does not mean that I wanted to pretend everything is fine. More like just wanting there to be a division between normal and abnormal or different. And, of course, that's the whole point: There really is no such division. The more I did open up to other people or listen out for their stories, the more I became aware that people did have bad experiences; parents got ill or died. The problem is that the world of Snapchat, TikTok or Instagram – whatever – that world has little space for sadness or difficulty. Or at least that's how it felt at the time. It's like showing just one face of life and the rest feels like something shameful, weak or vulnerable. Not really something to share too much.

Chapter 3

Anger is one letter short of danger

In the past week, Dad's finally got to speak to Mum's consultant after calling PALS and complaining that he did not yet have any updates. He tells me that the consultant has not put any gloss on things. Mum had serious trouble when the first EVD was positioned incorrectly and it had to be reinserted. There were infections and so on and eventually they needed to insert a shunt. The doctor gave Dad the prognosis that Mum would be hemiparetic (paralysed on her left side) and that she will have midbrain issues such as double vision and eye co-ordination problems that will persist. On the plus side, Mum survived the most critical period, and it will take some months before we know how much she will be able to recover.

That was hard to hear. Dad told me one morning after he had digested all this information. Before this update, we only had snatches of information. And I suppose the finality or certainty of that doctor's feedback was so stark. Up to that point, there was a vague hope that Mum would just be one of those exceptions to the rule. She's clever after all and

DOI: 10.4324/9781003171676-3

maybe she would make a miraculous recovery. She may still. But on the other hand, the doctor's update really helped since it was the first solid thing we had to hold on to. As if we could now recalibrate our hope within the new rules he had laid down.

We get to the ward, and it's an empty bed again. My heart jumps. Would they even have called us if she had died? It's possible that they could just forget her somewhere… after all, she would not be able to fend for herself if she were left somewhere in a corridor in this hospital. They should teach these skills somewhere: Hospital survival 101. Or maybe they just forget to call us. I can't help thinking of that night in A&E when it seemed as if we had to fill the gaps and prevent my mum from choking on her own vomit. Where is she?

They say Mum's been moved to a different ward, closer to a rehabilitation ward, but not yet there. Does this latest move mean that she's more "stable" now? When we get to the ward, we press the intercom, but no one comes. After 10 minutes, a nurse lets us in: "Ah yes, the intercom doesn't work…". I feel annoyed. Why have it then? I'm wondering why it can't be fixed. It seems such a waste for a nurse to leave whatever they are doing, just to come and open the door to relatives, who end up feeling guilty for disturbing the nurse.

In the ward, Léa almost jumps onto some other patient's bed – an older woman with sunken cheeks. She looks nothing like Mum and doesn't notice the intruder. My sister's getting so disoriented with all this moving about and seems to just want to settle down somewhere – preferably that first ward with all the shabby toys. Finally, we are surprised to see Mum, for the first time without the many tubes and monitors attached to her. She looks almost normal, as if nothing has happened. "Mummy!" my little sister squeals. I hug her, and my sister joins in. She tries to lift herself to hug us but doesn't quite manage. I think of how she always said she needs to hug us for us to grow. Someone had placed the television right up close to Mum's face and she was evidently watching some programme like *Antiques Roadshow* or some other thing she would never have watched before. She grew up without much television, and always loved a good book or audiobook if she's on the go. I shut the TV down for her. We all tell her about our days, that we miss her and try to explain what's happened – we don't know how much she actually remembers.

All the other patients here look like they've been in hospital since forever, like the ward is their home. They look ancient and frail. I realise a bit later on that it's mostly people who've had strokes that are in this ward. But there are also some younger people here. I wonder how long they've actually been here and how long my mum will be. There aren't any other visitors for any of the patients, like they've been forgotten. They are too quiet too, they sit in their beds, watching whatever TV program is streaming on the fold out tablets or lie in bed motionless, maybe asleep. Hopefully it's sleep.

It is "protected dinner time" on the ward. It seems a really strange choice of words – I wonder what's being protected? They are ferocious about us having to leave at this time. Previously Mum had been on a drip and was tube fed in the other wards but the nurse says that they did a "swallowing test" and now she's allowed to eat thickened mixtures. I look at the cup of "food" the nursing assistant is holding. Food is an overstatement. It looks like some sort of grey green goop, slightly more watery than jelly and semi-transparent. I try not to wrinkle my nose, but it's hard. And then I think: This is what keeps Mum alive here. If she can eat more normally, that's a step closer to coming home – perhaps. "It's apple today" the dinner lady says. This is apparently good news as my mum's eyes brighten. After saying goodbyes, we drive home late that night, all extremely tired but relieved. Even if Mum couldn't speak right now, we know that she's getting better, it will be slow for sure, but recovery is possible.

Our house is no longer our own. I come back from school, expecting the house to be empty. But instead, it's mayhem. Somehow my dad's colleagues had offered to come and help out with installing some stuff in the house, bookcases for the living room and so on. They're all here, arranging cupboards, building bookcases, working together. My godmother is among them. She works with my dad. They seem like one of those *DIY SOS* teams, all smiles and hard work. I smile at them and make small talk for a bit then slink off to my room. I can't even explain it, but it feels almost like anything out of the ordinary like this just reminds me again of how different our lives have become. It's like when the paramedics came into the house, all with a clear purpose. And then there's me – I feel purposeless, useless. I guess I should be downstairs helping them or something, but it feels too difficult. I retreat to my bedroom – it is mercifully untidy and all mine with no plans of being updated soon.

It is strange how we take things in our stride now. There's a girl in my year whose mother was going to have some operation or investigation in hospital soon and she was really worried about her mum. I say nothing when she leaves in a middle of a lesson, crying. I can't judge, but my "normal" is too important for me to ever let that happen to me. Even so, there's been more upheaval and Mum's back again in NCCU for a quick stopover after they had to remove her shunt to reposition it. Something had gone wrong with where they had previously placed it.

The operation to change the placement of Mum's shunt had gone well and she's back in the rehab ward. There's a bulge on her scalp and a nurse explains that this is where the shunt has now been placed. A chirpy nurse comes and goes and starts talking with Dad about Mum's personal care: Facial hair, leg hair… that kind of thing. I feel so embarrassed about this conversation, which feels all wrong. It's not supposed to be that way. But it turns out that there is an expectation that these things are simply taken care of by family or something. There is no real provision or expectation from nursing staff to deal with these things. I suppose that does make sense, they deal with life and death stuff. I wonder what would happen if no one ever did anything. Would Mum's fingernails grow to record proportions like that woman I once saw in the *Guinness Book of Records*?

And then things take on an even more embarrassing turn. Dad whips out some waxing strips and stuff from his bag. "You know, Tashi, I think we should just have a go…" – he means: "I expect you to have a go…". "Mum really was always very particular about her appearance you know, could you remove the hairs on her upper lip?". I wonder how long he had been carrying those wax strips around with him. Was he waiting for just this moment? Even if he doesn't say this, I feel the pressure and accusation from that little voice in my head – I suppose my conscience: *What's wrong with you? You should be the kind of daughter who does this yourself. Why can't you take some initiative? Do you not care about what matters to Mum?*

But I can't help myself: "Dad, it's not even that bad," I lie. It really is. Mum would stand with a little tweezer, pulling out facial hair sometimes. She was very particular about it. "But it's only peach fuzz really," I say – again not true. I feel angry and embarrassed, cornered. I don't even know why this is so difficult for me. Mum's just had surgery again; she probably has more serious things to worry about, if she could worry about them. I want to say to my dad that he should do it himself if he cares that much about it. But I realise that this would not be a good thing to say.

Reluctantly, I place one of the wax strips on her face. It's cold wax strips at least. I feel scared as well, as if I am doing a minor medical procedure. What if it upsets Mum or something goes wrong? Maybe some nurse would come and scold us – me – for upsetting or hurting her. Mum stares vacantly at me. I worry that I may hurt her. I take a deep breath and count down silently: 3…2…1 and rip! Nothing. Mum doesn't respond to this at all, although I think that her eyes may be smarting a little. Her eyes are big and open, like some kind of vulnerable animal – a fawn comes to mind.

I worry about what she thinks or understands about all of this and I can almost imagine her asking me: "Why are you hurting me?". I feel angry at my dad, at the nurse, and at myself. This is not what I ever imagined I would need to do and the absurdity of having to wax someone who has just had a life and death experience is not lost on me. I suppose life goes on. But this is hard. I can imagine other girls at my school going out with their mums to some spa and having all sorts of beauty treatments.

When we get home, my dad and my sister go off somewhere. I think my dad is angry at me for the fuss I made. Maybe he was even ashamed of me. He thinks that I have no idea of duty. At least he didn't keep harping on about how easy this all was in the end; maybe he found it as difficult as I did – he certainly seemed anxious about the whole hair removal thing. I suppose it's difficult to make decisions for someone in their best interest (you think), when they are not able to say what they would really like to happen. My dad sometimes talked about how difficult it can be to do things like clip the nails of your child or remove a splinter, especially if it is upsetting to the child. Although those things seem natural for a parent to do, waxing your unresponsive Mum felt a little different.

I get to spend a lot more time just on my own. It's like my dad has begun giving up on the idea of keeping up "normal" appearances with me tagging along unhappily. Maybe he's just giving up on me, so that he continues to try as hard as ever with my sister, but not with me. Saturdays seem busier than ever, and Dad keeps posting proud pictures of my sister now running the junior Park Run on Sundays. Onwards and upwards. I feel like I'm doing downwards and downwards, or maybe just... nothing. Although there are very minor variations, he thinks it's good for my sister to have some routine and predictability in her life and I can feel how he's trying to carve out some kind of "normal" existence away from the hospital.

But what can be more predictable than our trips to the hospital, our new "normal"? These trips seem about the only thing we still reliably do, other than school and work. For me, at least, the dog is always a good excuse for a walk or something and I wonder whether he also finds it difficult to be in the house too much. Other than my room, the rest of the house continues to feel uncomfortable – full of memories of Mum and also of the stroke. I feel uncomfortable when I get to the area where Mum first had the stroke. The backing of the stickies from the ECGs are still lying around in the room, even though Dad has hoovered the room a number of times. It's as if he doesn't quite want to remove them and keeps hoovering around them. I don't pick them up.

While my dad and sister are out, I just kind of idle. I draw, watch Netflix. I do nothing. Literally. Go down rabbit holes in Youtube. Daydream. Do stuff that feel pointless, feckless or even dumb. I can't really justify this, because the whole house is full of reminders of just how much there is to do and how much Mum always did. But it's like I can't will myself into action. Mum was always working so hard at everything: Top of her class, scholarships to Cambridge, boat races. And now she's stuck in a hospital bed. Does anything really have a point?

We're at the Heong gallery. For the first time in weeks, it feels like a normal family Saturday. A day in town which punctuates our otherwise non-normal half-life of hospital visits and exhaustion. Dad knows that I enjoy art and keeps telling me how I could make a career of it – I never believe him. But I enjoy this small gallery with this strange exhibition – *Half-boy* by Stuart Pearson Wright. I pause at the paintings which have a satisfying sense of menace and something sinister about them. It resonates with me. I pause in front of the painting of a boy walking away from a playpark in front of some ordinary looking red brick houses. He's holding his head and blood pours down his cheek. The horror lurking in everyday life. I take my time in front of the portraits of people looking at one another – expressionless. The exhibition makes me think about my life now: Danger seeps through many cracks in my world; menacing and dark things can escape through the cracks into my life. And then there's visiting, shopping, hair removal on the surface of it all. And you're left feeling hollow and pale with tiredness and sadness, just trying to avoid as many cracks as you can.

The head of year looks at me from across her desk, then to my dad – like we are strange specimens – we sit uncomfortably in the silence. She looks ready to pounce as she glares over her glasses: "I understand your situation is very difficult" – it sounds more like an accusation than commiseration. Long pause. It's that word "situation" again that I hate. Does everyone have a "situation" or is it just me? I suspect there are some other kids with "situations", and I never wanted to be one of them. She clears her throat, "The school would like to ensure that we support Tashi to the best of our abilities". Another pause, "So, we have decided that Tashi won't be doing the upcoming mock exams".

I relax a bit. This is amazing news – I have hardly had a second for schoolwork let alone revision. She goes on: "And we would like to offer you a meeting with the in-school counsellor – just to make sure you're fully supported". This is not so welcome news.

From what I understand of school counsellors, they are essentially robots which ask: "How does that make you feel?" to anxious twelve-year-olds. Maybe I shouldn't be so dismissive, I mean my dad is a psychologist after all and I guess I could use all the help I can get. I barely know how I feel, let alone how to deal with it.

Walking out of the school is strange. My dad seems annoyed at me… again: "Tashi you know that just because the school gave you a free pass on these mocks doesn't mean you can slack off." I nod, but he continues: "Seriously, you have to get into a good sixth form. If you don't do well on your GCSEs then – well, they follow you through your life". He is worried – he knows that I have found it difficult to really get into school-work much – even before the stroke. I know all of this. I know he's right. But, for some reason, it really annoys me – that he's talking like this, as if I've already failed. Maybe I am failing already. "The meeting went well though," I say as a kind of pacifier. He shrugs slightly, and we walk back to the car in silence. As we get close to home, we're both relaxed and the conversation flows like it did before Mum's stroke. We talk about that trip he had with me, taking just me to Turkey a year or two ago so that we can have a bit of little-sister free time together. Our more recent trip to South Africa (with Léa this time). It feels like these experiences will always be different from anything that comes now, after Mum's stroke.

It's Dad's birthday. My uncle from Canada is visiting and it feels almost like a normal birthday meal except for the gap at the dinner table where Mum would have sat. My dad was stoical and quiet about the whole thing. I made him a huge Victoria Sponge cake and helped my sister make a card. The cake came out much better than I expected, and I even found some old candles, gold paint not flaking too much, which I could re-use! When we light them and sing Happy Birthday with my uncle, I feel for a moment as if I had done something good: I have made a little bubble in which we could just *be*, instead of feeling as if we're on some kind of mission or some rushed visit.

Yesterday, Dad went to Mum on his own. I think he needs this sometimes, because when my sister and I are with him, he worries about us as well as Mum. He updates my uncle on what to expect. He's heard from my grandmother already, but Mum has been making a little progress and it is good to tell him about this.

We are asked to complete a lengthy communication profile for Mum, in which they ask all sorts of things about her preferences and background. It's almost like this did not really matter to them before now, so we take the sudden interest in Mum's actual background and preferences to be a good sign – a shift from crisis to rehab perhaps. It is strange to help Dad fill out the form and we laugh about items like: "18. Are there any topics of conversation that should be avoided?". Mum loves talking. She grew up in a house where there was good debate and she was part of a youth parliament in Canada, so I think that she would probably not want anyone to avoid any particular topics. I wonder what other people would put down for a question like that.

The next question makes me feel sad: "19. Is there anything they may particularly miss being able to do…?". What wouldn't Mum miss? I think of her hugs, of her cuddling our dog. Maybe she'd miss having a coffee; she would definitely miss now not being able to talk with people much, since this was one of the things she could do for hours. Dad's a bit stumped with the question and writes down something generic – talking to friends, chocolate…. He looks sad as he thinks of all the things Mum would probably have missed. I had a crazy thought that we should all perhaps get a form like this just in case anything happened to us, to save our family the difficulty of trying to answer for us.

It's back to turn taking again with my uncle and sister. When we visit Mum the next day, I notice the communication guidance pasted on a yellow sheet above Mum's bed. It says that Mum can nod or shake her head and that people should use short sentences with her. I ask my little sister to tell Mum what she's been doing with a family friend, who has been spending some time with her now and then. "No!" she says and leaves it up to me to explain. Mum stares intently but blankly at me as I explain the different crafts my sister has been busy with. She seems a little more able, like she was before all those operations that seem to have done more harm than good, and now manages a half-hug.

Mum now reaches up repeatedly with her right hand, something between a stretch and a reach. It happens a few times during a visit. Restless. It's like her arm has a life of its own. Probably making up for the lack of movement of her left arm. I wonder what it means, but sometimes just catch her hand as it comes down and hold it against my face. She doesn't seem to mind. My sister burrows into the bed like an insect. She is not in any way scared of this any longer and seems to enjoy the challenge of getting onto the bed. One or two nurses have sometimes murmured something about infection control, but generally they can't bring themselves to chase my sister off the bed. Léa is delighted when my uncle is in her relay team and when he takes her to the concourse, pretending that she's showing him around the hospital. I think she's so tired of me and Dad by now. Actually, my uncle doesn't even have to pretend that he's being shown around since my sister knows the place incredibly well and shows it off like any child would show off their home to a visitor. She now often runs ahead of us despite our best efforts to reign her in.

Mum has a tube in her nose, which the nurses say she keeps fussing with: "Oh they all do it", as if all patients have some kind of agreement to make nurses' lives even busier. She's got a kind of mohawk or punk hairstyle with a crew cut all around and longer hair on top. The hairstyle is the end product of all those drain and shunt operations that did not quite go to plan. Just before we go, I say: "Give me a kiss" and lean my head on her chest. I think she tries to lean forward a little but cannot yet make a kissing sound. I blow her a kiss as we leave, and she puckers her lips. She keeps them puckered too long as we say our goodbyes, as if she's forgotten that she was blowing a kiss.

When we get home, my dad asks me to help set up the Christmas tree. I know it's early in December, but I agree with him that we need Christmas and this would at least stop Léa from asking about when the tree goes up. After I assemble the tree, I come back to the living room to find my sister all dressed up in a velvety flower dress that looks Victorian. My uncle brought it from Canada. She's gently shaking one of the tree's branches and I stop myself before telling her not to do this: "I'm saying hi to the tree… I'm shaking it's hand," she says. Even if it's not a real tree, which we would prefer, this tree has endured many Christmases already in our family and we cannot get ourselves to get rid of it. My sister seems very pleased with the unfurling of Christmas things and is particularly excited about the fact that my uncle is here to help with making it feel a bit more like a fast-approaching holiday. But how will Christmas be without Mum here?

Sometimes when I wake up early, I go to the kitchen to find my dad already up. I think he runs on adrenaline and coffee these days. Léa is usually still sleeping and we have some time to ourselves. My dad talks about the different things he's worried about: "Tashi, did you see Mum's tongue? It's all covered with thrush or something I think… could be the blood sugars". I did notice.

That and Mum's dry lips, which my sister tried to "doctor" with some lip balm – she looked as if she was trying to colour Mum in. My dad talks about his concerns about Mum's blood sugars, which can skyrocket to 20 (whatever that means). I think back to my childhood when Mum's blood sugar was always there in the background. She would have a little bag with bits of blood-stained tissue from where she pricked her fingers to test her blood sugar. The smell of Insulin. The orange hypo box in the top drawer of the fridge she once taught me to use in case she had a serious blood sugar low. I can't really imagine Mum not being in control herself of her blood sugar. I am glad that Dad talks about these topics – safe ground. It's as if my dad and I share a common purpose. Safely far removed from other topics, like my obvious difficulty in doing much on my art portfolio for example.

There have been the periodic e-mails from my art teacher, which seem to upset Dad every time. One more thing he did not expect and cannot control. One more thing that should not be the way it is. He never seems to understand why or how I don't seem able just to get down and work on the art. I think some people can escape into work. Maybe I'm not one of them. And whatever he suggests to "help" actually just makes things worse. Well, not really worse, but it just makes me more anxious about something else I don't seem able to do much about. It's bad enough that the teacher is offering lunch time "sit ins" and after school sessions to make sure that my projects keep progressing. Another place where I can't just be.

"I have followed advice and written to PALS," Dad says. He is irritated that he had to contact them again, this time in writing, but some of the nurses suggested that he should do this. He explains how he complained to them about Mum's diabetes manage-ment (which is done by a different team) and how some nurses were really worried about how difficult it was to control Mum's blood sugar. It seems so odd that different departments don't even talk to one another in the same hospital, let alone talk with family of the patient.

Dad explains that he has had another "battle" – this time about Mum's physiotherapy: She has these splints which she is supposed to wear on her left lower arm and on her leg, but I've never actually seen them on her. They just lie about around her bed. I think back to a recent visit when Dad uncurled Mum's fingers on her left hand and saw how the nails had been digging into the palm of her hand because they had grown too long. Mercifully he actually cut them instead of asking me to do this and also buffed them for her. I told him that he could have a different career as manicurist, although he would draw a line at pedicures for sure. Mum has to wear these splints on and off, otherwise her hand and foot will become too spastic to use and those fingernails will just keep digging deeper into the palm of her hand.

This is the first time I see Mum with anything get-ting close to a smile – or for that matter an expres-sion. It's not much, but it's better than the slightly scared look she sometimes has. She's finally been moved onto a rehabilitation ward which does feel very different from the previous more medical wards. There is actually a "programme" of activities posted above Mum's bed, which suggests that she sometimes goes to a gym and so on. She looks tired when we see her, but smiles! But we're not there for long when a doctor comes to tell us: "We're a bit worried about Karen and she will be moving to R2 now, just as a precaution, so that we can check out why her bloods show some infection". The doctor explains that Mum may have sepsis and I have a sinking feeling about this – everywhere, even on some ambulances – I have seen warnings about sepsis and how severe it is.

As we drive home, Dad tells me and my sister the Zen parable about the Chinese farmer, who never gets happy or sad in the face of all the challenges he has, because we never know whether something will be a good or bad thing in the end. I really am beginning to feel like that, because it feels as if every step forward for Mum is met by an equal small step back which reminds us just how slow progress really is and which also reminds us never to get too euphoric about any progress, which may be short lived.

Despite Mum's quick stay in a different ward, today she's made it back to the rehab ward again. Mum also follows conversations much better it seems, even if she still doesn't really speak. Dad did this imagery exercise with her and asked her to close her eyes and imagine that she is walking up to and into our house: "You're at the front door... you open it and see the floor tiles and smell the house smells...".

He walked Mum through the entire house this way and at the end I saw her tear up a little when she opened her eyes when the walk through was all done. I can't imagine how much she must wish she was home now, almost two months after her stroke.

It's the day of my sister's Christmas musical at school. In the end we dressed her up as a shiny bauble in a beautiful sequin dress my dad and uncle bought for her. I arrive just in time for the show – *The X-mas factor*. It is hard to be here. It does not feel like Christmas to me. Families are packing the place out: I see mums, dads, grandparents in the audience. Our family feels so thin on the ground. Just me and my dad. The out of tune finale makes me feel both happy and sad at the same time as the children chorus: "All I want for Christmas is yooooouuuuu". I am not sure what I want for Christmas – obviously Mum never to have had a stroke. I can't think of anything else I would want.

When we get to the hospital the next day, Dad asks my sister to sing the songs they sang at *The X-mas factor* to Mum. She needs lots of encouragement and eventually sings a snatch or two from one of the songs. Mum looks intent but unsmiling. The whole bay is bathed in yellow light, making all of us look a little ill… "It's time for us to come together" my sister sings thinly. There is nothing of the previous day's exuberance or vibe and I wonder whether the hospital should start piping Christmas music into all the wards just to make things a little happier for everyone.

It's eight days before Christmas and I think that I have actually had my gift today. Mum smiles broadly at me when I hug her. Even her eyes are smiling at me. I am holding the iPad up to Mum, while trying to help her use an app designed to help people with aphasia communicate. Even with prompting, Mum struggles to press the bright icons, which don't all seem to link to what they're trying to say. "Try this one, Mum," I suggest, pointing at some of the emotion faces. Everything seems to take such a long time for Mum. "Ready... bored... angry" the electronic voice intones as she presses some random icons. It is clear that she is engaged but it's quite beyond her. Well, we're giving it a try, I think to myself while wondering whether this is ever going to work. Repeatedly, Mum presses an icon with a cheetah on it. "Oh, it's a joke see...," I explain. The voice intones: "Why should you not play cards in the jungle? There are too many cheetahs...". Even with my help, the app is not much use in helping Mum make herself more understood. Maybe she pressed the cheetah because it made her think of Léa in the cheetah suit Mum had made for her. It is like playing a very bad game of charades where you never really get the answer in the end. I thought the app would do the trick and that Mum would be telling us whatever she needed to, a bit like Stephen Hawking. But a more worrying thought is that she may not actually be able to think of anything to communicate.

The three of us huddle together on Christmas Eve around Mum's bed. Her red communication folder is

on her lap and she seems very pleased with what Dad
has put together for her team. It's really just some
photos of things and people that matter to her. I
notice that she can now page through it herself and
that she seems engrossed in it. She has a new blue
Christmas scarf that hides the pink hospital pyjamas
and family friends have dropped off a little Christmas
tree that stands on her side table. My sister's child-
minder, who is also a music therapist in training,
comes to visit while we are with Mum, and she starts
strumming the guitar. She is so calm as my sister
starts hitting the strings now and then at her invita-
tion. A little later, I borrow the guitar and play
something I used to play better. I can't remember
when last I picked up my guitar and played anything.

It is Christmas Day and we try as best we can to
include Mum in all the gifts and silliness that we
shared at home. We are surprised when the nurses
suggest that we can take Mum out of her bed in a
wheelchair. It's more like a giant wing back chair
with wheels, and I can see that Dad feels nervous at
first at making this first trip out of Mum's room with
her, but we manage to take Mum to the dining room
which immediately satisfies my sister since it at least
has a polar bear dressed up as Father Christmas and
a larger Christmas tree in the corner. It feels so different to see Mum in a chair rather than in bed.

It's 31st December. Normally the kind of time
when you're thinking about the New Year and what
you wish different. We arrive at the hospital to find
out that Mum has had a fall. It's awkward since

there's nowhere private to have the discussion and we talk in front of Mum, almost as if she were not there. A nurse tells us that they used the wrong type of therapy chair (one without a constraint) and that Mum was left unattended for a bit because they have staff shortages. I can see how Dad battles with being understanding and angry at this oversight. He asks whether they know how badly Mum was injured and the nurse tells us that she did not hit her head, but that there is a bruise on her side. Nothing broken, but they will request X-rays just to be on the safe side, although a junior doctor has checked her over. When Dad asks her how long Mum lay there before someone discovered that she had fallen, she mumbles something vague but doesn't answer. Too long; who knows how long? They're thin on staff during the holidays.

It is New Year's Day. Dad dragged Léa and me out for a morning run (his New Year's resolutions) and after recovering from the run, we're at the hospital. Even though it's protected mealtime, the nurses allow us to stay with Mum throughout the meal. We find out that Mum is very tired and that she had a busy day. The X-rays confirmed that she was unharmed from the fall. The occupational therapist has pushed Mum to do as much of her own personal care as possible (washing her face, brushing her teeth). It's difficult to think that this is too exhausting for Mum. We spent a long time with Mum and the iPad as she seemed to want to tell us something. After about thirty minutes of guessing, typing and more guessing, we worked out that Mum had written "Nurse D" and when we quizzed her more on this, it seemed as if she wanted Dad to contact the diabetic nurse. It makes sense since this has always been Mum's biggest concern: Managing her blood sugars.

The new year brings with it quite a lot of changes: Mum can now actually whisper. I was the first to make this out when I said that I loved her and heard her whisper back a breathy "I... love... you". My other uncle is visiting – also from Canada – and Mum was able to whisper "I love you" to him too. Mum's neatly coloured rehabilitation timetable seems to be getting fuller, and it feels like the nurses know her and relate more to her as a person rather than a patient.

I wonder whether she could write something, and I hold up our visitors' book for her. It takes a long time, but eventually she writes: "Ask" in a shaky hand. Half an hour of questioning does not reveal what she wanted us to ask or of whom. Dad asks her if she was in pain and she says: "All over". I suspect she meant that she was in pain all over, which is a terrible thought. But then again, maybe she meant that she no longer had the pain and that it was all *over*. The low point of this visit – there's usually a low point – comes when a speech and language therapist explains to Mum and Dad that she needs to get a "PEG" (percutaneous endoscopic gastrostomy) tube which will be fitted to her stomach and through which they will be able to give her mushy food and liquids instead of trying to feed her by mouth, which risks choking. Mum looks worried as they talk about this next step for her. "It feels a little like giving up," Dad later tells me. He thinks that one reason for the PEG is that it would help them to discharge Mum sooner, which may not be a good idea.

Again, to my embarrassment, the issue of Mum's beauty care comes up. A chirpy little auxiliary nurse tells us that she gave Mum a "spa" treatment and on further questioning, she tells us that it's not too difficult to shave Mum's legs and that I should definitely do it. I am terrified at the thought, imagining nicking Mum's legs everywhere and blood gushing onto her hospital bed. The nurse is really keen on the blood sugar monitoring device which Dad has managed to link up to Mum's phone. It reads her blood sugars continuously and sends him updates via an app, so that he can see just how well or how poorly her blood sugar is being controlled. I think he would really like the hospital to use this monitor instead of constantly pricking Mum's fingers for blood, as this seems a little upsetting to her. But we soon learn that there are set protocols and that too many clever ideas are not met with enthusiasm.

This is the first time we actually take Mum out of the ward in a wheelchair. I am the one pushing the chair and instead of feeling happy or excited, I feel terrified of ramming her legs into doors or other obstacles or bumping into someone equally frail in the busy concourse. My uncle is with us. I don't allow myself to feel embarrassed, but it is tougher than I thought. I am aware of some glances as we make our way to Costas and imagine I can hear things like: "What happened to her?" or "Poor little one" when they see my sister. It is so hard for me to feel as if we're on display and I wheel the chair into a quiet corner of Costas. At the same time, I feel angry at myself for being self-conscious. Despite my uncle's unwavering smile and optimism, this is not easy: Mum soon seems agitated and she's not allowed to drink coffee. Dad spoons some cappuccino foam into her mouth. He gives Mum some of my hot chocolate in a spoon. It's not a good idea and Mum coughs a little, as if she's almost choking on the little liquid we give her. The noise and activity around us, even in this dark corner, is overwhelming to all of us, let alone to Mum and I've not even drank half of my hot chocolate when we have to rush back to the ward. Mercifully my uncle pushes the wheelchair. It is a relief to get back to the ward.

Somehow it is almost protected dinner time by the time our outing is over. My sister eyes one of the pots of yoghurt handed out by the woman who manages feeding the patients. After our outing, I understand some of the anxiety surrounding such mealtimes better. We dash out before being shooed out. When we return, Mum tries to speak – a kind of continuous mumble but more than whispering. She actually says: "Hi Tashi". My sister is delighted to find an uno-pened yoghurt which she is allowed to eat. I tell her not to squiggle around so much and not to spill yoghurt over Mum. Am I turning into a parent? It does not take long for Léa to finish off her yoghurt and to end our visit by belting out a song she makes up on the spot for Mum, who leans back, eyes closed: "Can I stay here all day or night... no matter how the food tastes... I love you, so can I stay... I want to stay. Please can I stay?". Mum looks at her but does not respond and we leave.

We're getting ready for a trip to Glasgow, for Dad's postgraduate neuropsychology course. Just a day or so before leaving for Glasgow, he attended a case conference with all of Mum's staff – occupational therapist, physiotherapist, dietician, rehabilitation consultant and many more. "It took 77 days for anyone to sit down and actually tell me what is going on for Mum," he says. He found out that we were supposed to have had some co-ordinator assigned to us, but that this person had been on sick leave and that we had "slipped through the cracks". Maybe there is no such person, since none of the other families we come across ever mention having such a co-ordinator either.

The different people involved in Mum's care packed out the room. He told me that it was stressful and that the way forward is very confusing, with the possibility that Mum would need rehabilitation far away from where we live in a specialist unit. There's a lot else that came from the meeting: They suggest –as if we should have known it – that we bring in clothes for Mum, so that she no longer has to wear hospital gowns. There's even a goal of working on Mum's ability to sit up for two hours or so, so that it may become possible to do short trips into Cambridge with her.

We go clothes shopping for Mum – everything has to be oversized, loose, cool (the hospital is always overheated). It's the strangest shopping trip and if I weren't so stressed about it, I would have felt embarrassed, with Dad holding huge bits of clothing up against himself asking whether it would fit Mum and with my little sister weaving in and out of racks of clothing evidently playing the best game of hide and seek she has ever played. We arrive later the day at the hospital with all the clothing. I show each item to Mum, who struggles to pay attention. She is irritable and glowers at the other patients opposite her. A nurse tells us that Mum has not liked being in the therapy chair recently. No wonder: She fell! Maybe she's angry because the other patients didn't help or call for help – they can't of course. Dad tries to explain to Mum that we are going to be away for a while in Glasgow, for his course. He started the course just before Mum had the stroke. I don't think she has any idea that this means it will be a week and a half before we see her again.

Dad actually had to take me and my sister out of school since there was no one who could look after us and we could not have stayed alone at home. Actually, I probably could have. But it's just as well I came along since he obviously needs someone to look after my sister and I needed to get out. We have an incredible Airbnb flat –high ceilings, comfortable and uncluttered. During the day, Dad's on his course which seems very demanding. He cycles off in the rain to a hospital and comes back when it's almost dark. My sister and I have developed a routine of going for a walk among the squirrels on the way to the Botanical Gardens. Each time we go, we share crumbs and seeds with them and one actually sat on my hand once. I am beginning to understand why my dad and sister frequent the botanical gardens in Cambridge.

The dog stays with us and seems delighted with the trip. Over the weekend, we go to Dumbarton Castle. It is surprising that we get there, since Mum always did the navigating. It is wonderfully windy when we explore around the castle and I feel as if I can take off into the air like a kite into a wind that seemed to blow away all my thoughts and worries. This trip feels like a holiday. It feels like I can be somewhere in that space between child and grown up again. We have had some FaceTime calls with Mum and Mum's keyworker has been updating us in e-mails about her progress. This does feel very different from Mum's time in hospital so far. Our days blur into one – dark, cold, squirrels, art galleries, weekend sightseeing. When we visit the Glasgow Science Centre, I get stuck in front of a simulation, which takes a snapshot of you then shows how you will age. I add all the risk factors: Drinking, smoking, overeating. The face that stares back at me doesn't look great, but it looks how I feel: Blotchy, frowny, dishevelled. Inevitably my dad comes over: "You see, that's why you shouldn't do that stuff… Your future self will thank you". Yeah, if I have a future self!

We get the occasional photo message from Mum's team. Mum is not able to send any texts or pictures herself. I'm looking at the latest one of Mum actually standing during a gym session. She is surrounded by four white shirted physios and OTs and her key-worker beams up at her. A physiotherapy assistant stands behind her. Her hair is short, as if she's either very alternative or as if she's survived something serious. Mum is beaming and the whole scene reminds me of a portrait of a saint we saw Edinburgh – her therapists looking like astonished disciples as they crouch around her admiringly. It is a big moment, but I catch myself before I hope for too much.

We're back in the hospital with Mum, who is dressed for the occasion in her own clothes instead of the pink hospital pyjamas. Glasgow already feels very far away as I ask my sister: "Tell Mummy about the squirrels we saw". Incredibly, Mum says: "Did you see squirrels?". It is nasal; not quite her voice – child-like and monotonous. But she's a different person from the one we left in the ward less than a fortnight ago. Maybe we're the problem – tiring her out or something, so that she's had time to actually recover. I can't believe the change. I also cannot believe that I have to go back to school and that we had actually been away.

We're laughing out loud. Mum is sitting in a wheelchair with a faulty headrest. The staff nurse commented that the design has been faulty for the past 20 years. Immediately, Mum told him he should come up with a better one. That's the engineer in her coming through. When we tell him Mum's not that kind of engineer – she is a theoretical mechanical engineer – he understands why she declines to fix the chair herself with the Allen keys he joked about bringing in. Moments like this make me feel hopeful – as if Mum is going to make a really good recovery.

As we walk into the ward today, we can hear Mum talking to someone when we are still outside her bay. But when we get to her, there's no one with her. She talks to no one in particular. It makes me feel sad and bewildered. Maybe she's lonely? Is she hallucinating? One of the nurses mention to my dad that she has been talking to herself in this way for a while now and that the woman at the opposite end of the room has family who complained about this. I can see the embarrassment and rage my dad feels; I feel the same. Just because their mum or whoever she is, sleeps most of the day doesn't mean that she won't also start talking to no one in particular one day. Of course, it will be difficult with so many very ill people packed into a small space. But Dad makes light of it with Mum: "You've got so much to say today! It's best to keep it all for us though… You've always loved chatting".

I feel uneasy though and not so optimistic. Mum now has the PEG tube fitted and it's very strange to see a tube protruding straight from her stomach and a bag of brownish mush draining itself directly into her stomach. Doesn't she miss the taste of stuff like chocolate? She had a particular relationship with Bournville bars which she squirrelled away. I'm lost in these thoughts when Mum says she wants to tell me something. But the nurses come around and tell us that they will be giving her a bed bath which should only take ten minutes or so. We've learned from before and come back more than half an hour later.

They're just finishing off and my sister is beyond herself and done with waiting. I go to get chairs for us to sit on – there are only about six chairs in the whole ward and even those are difficult to locate. After a while of awkward chair sourcing, I come back, and the nurses are gone. My sister and my dad are standing by the bed. "Tashi" my mum says, her voice sounding robotic and monotone. "Hi Mum, how are you," I say with a forced smile, she looks distressed. "The nurses are trying to kill me," she says. I look at my dad – confused – he seems as lost as I am.

"Karen," he says softly, "What do you mean by that? Could you explain?". She shifts slightly, "Yes." A long pause as she gathers her thoughts: "They took me to a farm last night and tonight they are going to shoot me". I don't know what to say. I mean what do you say? My mother has gone mad. She seems weirdly calm about it though, like it's just a fact and I suppose it isn't much crazier than what's already happened… "Has something happened? Are you worried about getting hurt?" My dad asks, again. Now he does sound like a psychologist, calm and reasonable; I can hear that he's careful not to suggest anything. Maybe he has the chair incident in mind; maybe that's what she's upset about.

"No," Mum answers simply, "but they're going to shoot me tonight". I feel sorry for the nurses, God, I hope they don't overhear her, or they might actually be tempted, with all the hard work they've done to keep her comfortable. "I don't think they are trying to kill you, Karen, their job is to make sure you're safe…". She looks angrily at my dad, cutting him off: "No. Listen! You don't listen to me! They are going to kill me!". She is angrier at him for not listening than at them for wanting to kill her. I know they aren't going to hurt her in any way but the way she talks is so certain, she's clearly very angry at my dad for having even questioned it.

We try to change the topic a few times; she isn't going to change her mind and there isn't any way we can make her feel better about it. It's hard to find things to think of though. Before the stroke it was so easy to talk to her, she would always understand me or at least try to, and she'd listen to me, actually listen. Now I don't know what to say. If she didn't have a stroke, I'd probably have talked about how I'm so scared about my grades, but I feel paralysed, like I don't have the willpower to try, like I'm destined to fail. Or that I'm worried about Dad, he's so stressed about work and money, and I feel like I can't talk to him like I used to with her. I'd tell her how I miss her, how nothing's the same anymore and even though I know she isn't dead there's still a massive gap in my life. When we leave, we can hear Mum still talking to herself.

Mum keeps on saying things that sound completely crazy like: "I'm missing in action" or "I am off at the farm again". It is disconcerting, but also a bit of a mystery and I feel proud of myself when I tell Dad that I figured out that she is taking bits and pieces of conversations that she hears, or nursing banter, and that she seems to believe these things. It dawned on me when I overheard a nurse saying: "Oh, she's missing in action" to a family member, referring to their sleeping relative.

The next day I have an appointment with the school counsellor. I'm attending it so that I can say that I have attended it. It's my hall pass, my ticket out of the mocks – as was made very clear to me. I would never hear the end of it if I didn't. The only kids I've ever seen going to her are the ones who eat lunch with the cleaning ladies. The counsellor does not have an actual office. It's literally not much bigger than a cupboard and has a small round table and two uncomfortable plastic school chairs. No windows, only a neon light. I imagine it's not too different from the back office in a bar. I've heard of a girl with panic attacks who came to counselling for a while and I have no idea how someone with panic attacks could actually be in this little space. It's possibly one of the most awkward silences of my life, she sits there expectantly as if I'm supposed to validate her poor career choice. She nudges a box of tissues a bit closer and begins: "So… your mum had a stroke about a month ago?".

"Almost three months…".

She smiles as if she had just accomplished some massive breakthrough, "Ah right, and how are you

feeling?" I stare at her blankly – a look I've culti-
vated. Would it be too far to say I feel like I want to
leave? Probably. "I'm feeling OK I guess." "Oh, that's
great to hear!" – it sounds like I'm letting her off the
hook or something. Maybe she doesn't really want to
see me either and just wants to keep doing whatever
she does in this little office on her own. I shift
uncomfortably. I don't want to tell her anything let
alone stuff I don't want to admit to myself.

"How is school going?" she asks. School? That's a
joke, I mean I've barely had three seconds to sit down
let alone actually accomplish anything productive and I
think even if I did have the time, I probably wouldn't do
anything because – I mean – what's the point? Shall I
tell her about Mum's academic career? Rowing for
Cambridge? Should I tell her I feel like just taking a gap
year or maybe a gap decade right now if I could? I've
given it serious thought, starting my career as a run-
away teenager. "School's fine. I'm getting on top of
things. The teachers are all helpful," I tell her what she
needs to hear. I am good at this, and she seems unable
or unwilling to dig much. I walk out of the office not
much later than I wanted to.

I feel like those cops on TV who need a check-up
before they can return to duty. Apparently, I've got
the all-clear, the school's mental health verification
check, a gold star for showing up. Great. Maybe I
should have been honest, told her how impossible
everything feels, how I'm just lost and tired all the
time, and nothing makes sense. But then what,
another meeting? Or maybe she'll end up getting a

panic attack or something in that little office and then I'll end up having to look after her. No, I will never go into that damp little closet again – at least not unless I actively want to pursue a future as a mental health patient.

We are outside in the hospital garden with Mum for the first time. It tries so hard to be an actual garden, hemmed in by the hospital, and it actually almost succeeds. At least it's a clear day; there are snowdrops (it's February after all) and we've brought our dog along. He's perching a bit uncomfortably on Mum's lap, but seems really serious, as if he realises he should try not to scare or hurt her. I really wish I could know his thoughts at this very moment. Mum seems delighted to see him. Dad is stressing about everything. Mum has a wonky footplate on her wheelchair and at one point her left foot slipped off the wheelchair and actually dragged underneath it before we realised. Luckily no harm done, although we mention it to the nurses afterwards. When we take Mum back to the ward, she is so tired but after being settled in bed, she sings *Seven little rabbits* to my sister, who looks really tired. Mum remembers the words but sings drowsily and out of tune and falls asleep long before finishing the song.

Today Dad takes me to my first choice for my Sixth Form College. It it's a redbrick building with an excellent reputation. I pretend to be confident but think: There is no way I am getting in here. I am interviewed by one of the counsellors – no idea why. We make our way to her office along a curved, modern passage which contrasts with the tile floors and worn wood of the rest of the school. The counsellor at my school would probably not know what to do with herself in an office like this, with its strategically placed tissues and inviting chairs. She touches tactfully on the situation with Mum and assures us that they have excellent pastoral care. That would probably be the last reason why I would choose any college over any other college. I am glad to exit the curvy passageway into the normality of the rest of the school.

By chance, we meet my best friend and her parents. I am all smiles, hugs and excitement, but can't shake being aware of a sense of anger and sadness, like a scratchy label in a shirt. We go out and grab huge Subway sandwiches which I hide behind, listening to my friend's big plans for her future in the school.

When we see Mum at the hospital, I tell her about my subject choices and inevitably forget some. I feel stupid and embarrassed – don't even know what subjects I am interested in. I can sense that Mum would have liked me to take Maths, like she did. Clumsily, I change the topic to "half birthdays" since Mum was always the one who kept track of these things. Impressively, she knows all the dates of upcoming half birthdays. "Maybe I should make a half cake and wear a half dress on my half birthday!" I say. "No! Don't do that!" Mum seems genuinely angry at the thought. I explain that I was only joking, but she still seems a little annoyed at me.

At the hospital we meet my mum's physiotherapist, we've seen her before but today she seems more serious than normal and asks to have a conversation with my dad. I don't think much of it, I've gotten used to not particularly caring, it makes everything very easy. When he comes back, he seems disappointed. "What was that about?" I ask. "She just wanted to discuss Mum's future – with rehab –" he pauses, "it's looking more and more like she will not walk soon... not walk again". I frown, how could they say that when it's only been half a year? And she's already got better, I mean for starters she's actually awake and she can talk.

We get back to Mum. It would crush her to hear what the physiotherapist had to say. She asks, "When am I coming home?". I look to my dad, he doesn't answer but we both know that if ever, it will be a long time. Our house is a fixer-upper that needs *DIY SOS* or something; as soon as Dad fixes one part of it, everything else crumbles. In fact, Dad has actually applied twice to the television show *DIY SOS* after his colleagues suggested this, but we've heard nothing back from them. For us it really is do it yourself. Even if Mum could walk around easily, we'd have to do a lot of work before she could come home – and now that they're saying she will never walk again... well, it just seems impossible.

I feel useless, I hate that I can't do anything to help her, she's my mother for God's sake, she has looked after me every day of my life and now that she needs me, I'm paralysed. I reach out and hold her hand, it's her left one which she still can't feel. It must be so terrifying for her every day. They say the area of the brain which was worst affected is the thalamus, apparently, it's a highway for all the information you get from your senses and controls how you perceive the world – even whether you are awake or asleep. Maybe that's why she says those crazy things, talking about how the nurses are trying to kill her. Maybe all those things feel like they are happening. I think it's like her brain creating a metaphor for how she feels when she doesn't really want to admit it, or maybe she can't admit it. She's trying to say that she feels scared, and she doesn't know what's happening – she doesn't know what to be scared of either, so she pretends, it's much safer to be scared of a human than to admit that you're terrified of your future. Or maybe they've just drugged her up on something a bit too strong for her. At least Mum names what she's afraid of. I don't know what I'm scared of anymore. Maybe I'm not scared of anything, or maybe everything is so scary my brain decided not to bother with fear. I try to remember the last time I was scared, probably when she had the stroke though at that point, I was more concentrated on her surviving. Now I think I'm the one still just trying to survive.

Things are not really settling down for Mum. On Valentine's Day, she seemed all Valentined out by the time we got to see her: "She's got an eight legged lover..." Mum was talking at the top of her voice about the sweet old lady opposite her, who really did not look as if she had any kind of lover. My dad was utterly confused about this statement. It seems important to both of us that we try to puzzle out the sense in Mum's madness and finally we made sense of it: The woman opposite Mum had a big, black furry blanket on top of her and it actually did look a lot like some giant spider sitting on top of her. Could it be that Mum thought that was her lover? The visits have a very different feel from the early days when Mum was unresponsive or couldn't talk much. Now, we never know what to expect next from her.

Today, when we get to the ward, there seems to be a bit more activity than usual. A nurse tells us Mum is making cards in the dining hall. Why? I wonder: Christmas is over; Valentine's has gone. Why does Mum have to make cards? Wasn't Valentine's Day enough? I think, wondering whether "Spiderman" is going to feature again. Mum's occupational therapist intercepts us – she's energetic like a little robin and seems delighted that my sister and I are here: "Why don't you two come and join us?". I can feel the pressure and embarrassment: We'd be sitting with Mum and the other ten or so clients around a large round table. Some of them seem fast asleep and drooping dangerously into the glitter already. Also, crafts can be challenging with my sister, but she's already joining in, scattering buttons and glitter everywhere. "Show Tashi the card you're working on, Karen!" the OT suggests. Mum holds up a bright red card with a large plastic pearl on the front. It's minimalist for sure. I think Mum tried to write something on the card – I can't make it out. We used to have the same handwriting.

I sit down with Mum and try to help her decide what else she wants to put on the card. I try to steady her hand and help her write but it's so frustrating for her. Léa looks at the card Mum has created, then back to hers. She's written Mum on hers and pasted flowers and a tree onto hers – quite artistic really. I help Mum stick some lace flowers onto the card. She thumbs a lace skull, which I paste on as well. We've made a card for a really weird occasion here: flowers and skull. Mum is getting really fidgety, and we end up going to a quieter seminar room, where we try to finish the cards off. Dad asks us to hold the cards up for a photo and Mum is really not happy: "It looks like what a child would do," she says. She would never have said this in front of my sister before. Dad saves the moment by beginning to sing "It's tidy time", with Mum joining in. She is momentarily happier. Easily distracted.

The seminar room has an unplugged computer keyboard lying around. I show Dad, who enthusiastically shows Mum: "Look, Karen! Maybe you can try this to write things down with". I know that he's thinking that the iPad has been very tricky and that a keyboard may work better. She starts stabbing at it with her index finger but soon becomes furious: "You're tricking me! Stop it! You're mean!". She stabs at what seems just the right half of the keyboard. I feel frazzled as we wheel her back to the bay. It feels good to head off home today as it felt whatever we tried to do for Mum ended up just frustrating her. After saying goodbye to Mum, Dad and I work out that Mum must not be seeing half of the keyboard and that she doesn't understand this.

I ask my dad what the nurse said about phy-siotherapy. I don't think he wants to talk about it really, but he explains that they are now thinking of sending her to a different rehabilitation hospital. That sounds like good news surely. "Yes, it is. The only issue is that it's in London," he explains. Oh, I guess that wouldn't be so bad, I love London and we used to go all the time, it's a city full of potential and bursting with life and if going there would mean Mum gets better care then that would be amazing. "It would be, but it would mean we can only see her on weekends, and we don't actually know if she's going to get a place, it's very selective." Maybe it wouldn't be so bad just going on weekends, at the moment we're visiting almost every day and as much as I love seeing my mum and I know it's so impor-tant, it's difficult to balance everything. Even though we live a short drive away from Mum's hospital, it can take long before we park and actually get to spend time with her. I can't imagine how long it will take if we need to visit her in London.

Today, Mum is as sharp as ever: She tells us about a chaplain visiting her and says: "It was freaky!". Dad asks her to explain more, and she says that he sang badly and that he tries to convince people of what he believes. "Mmmm... tell us more about him... Was he clever?" Dad asks. I'm not sure where he's going with this, but Mum enjoys the conversa-tion: "No... he was not clever. You can tell by the eyes!". Even Léa joins in. Mum never suffered fools gladly. I can't imagine how frustrated this clever woman must be with people who talk with her as if she's a child.

We get a text message from a Canadian friend of Mum's. She tells how she brought some maple syrup cookies back from Canada and asked whether Mum wanted to give them to her team. Mum eagerly agreed and when they got to the gym, she belted out: "O Canada" – the Canadian National Anthem. She did not waver or stop until she had sung the whole thing word (if not note) perfect. Finally, we get to see Mum in a gym session with her physiotherapist. She is sitting up with the help of a rehab assistant while her physiotherapist holds up a big yellow bucket for her. She has to put little orange cones into the bucket and does this one by one. She smiles when she manages to get them into the bucket which the physiotherapist slowly moves around. The physio gets her to "row" with a bright blue baseball bat. Mum leans forward and pulls back a few times when her right hand slips. She angrily snaps at him – it is so uncharacteristic and over as quickly as it came… my mum rowed for Cambridge and beat Oxford in the annual women's boat race. My face flushes – the same feeling I had when we were making those cards.

It's good to visit Mum and actually not do anything much. We're watching the movie *Sing* and Mum and my sister are completely glued to it. My sister is getting annoyed though, because Mum keeps talking to the animated characters as if she's actually a cast member herself. When disaster strikes in the movie, she gets so upset that Dad offers to turn the movie off, even as my sister protests. The show goes on. As the depressed Koala in the movie hides away from his friends, Dad asks Mum: "Do you want to help him?". She answers: "I want him to be OK". It feels like Mum can no longer filter out real from unreal, although it's also good to see that she can at least lose herself in a story. That must be an important skill if you're trapped in a hospital bed all day long. Also, it is *so* Mum to be empathic towards the downtrodden Koala bear. She has always been a great listener and carer. It feels good to see these aspects of her emerge as she gets better.

I'm staring at the mirror. I have spots all over my face and can't believe that I got chicken pox. My sister brought it back from school a month or so ago and she's already recovered. Magic skin. I feel angry at her – I shouldn't, but I do. I look terrible and feel terrible. I lie on the kitchen tile floor covered with a grey woolly blanket. The dog lies next to me – I swear he knows I'm ill. Léa sits next to me with her doctor's kit and presses plastic medical instruments into my face, mouth and ears. She says she will make me feel better before she has to leave for school. I am too ill to argue with her, but thankful when the doctoring has to end, and my dad and sister rush off to her school. Later, the doorbell rings. There is no way that I will be opening it for anyone. I look and feel too bad, grotesque even. It's a close friend of my dad's, with his daughter. I look at the text again, which tells me that Dad is planning to make dinner for them when he's back from work and that I should "just let them in". I ignore the doorbell and hide away. Somba barks but I hush him, dragging him into the kitchen with me. I muffle his barking by hugging him. The doorbell stops ringing. A while later they must have come back because it starts ringing again. This time I don't even get up, I just hug the dog closer. I wonder how he would look if he got chicken pox. Do dogs even get chicken pox? I know that my dad will be massively disappointed in me, because he makes a big deal about hospitality. I don't care today. I'm not sure I really ever want to leave the house. Will I have these scars on my face for life? It's a new low for me.

I am just beginning to recover from the chicken pox and the hospital has given me the all-clear for visiting Mum again. Dad's been going on his own, because of the risk of spreading chicken pox. When we get to Mum's bed, I see that the poster Dad made is still up. It still exclaims: "Thank you for everything you do for me. Merry Christmas and a Happy New Year!". It's probably time to take it down, but I leave it there for now. I imagine the poster following Mum around wherever her rehab next takes her. Forever stuck in Christmas and New Year. Hopefully everyone now just thinks I have bad acne instead of chicken pox. I feel so self-conscious and wonder whether anyone notices that I am only wearing hoodies now so that I can clam up like an oyster when I feel too fragile. My sister is talking to Mum, sharing her plans for how we can adapt the house for her: "The stairs can be escalators," she points out.

Mum is unfocused and her delusions seem worse than ever. It seems cruel that, just as she seems to be making some progress, she has to struggle with more difficulties. This time neither Dad nor I could actually ground her statements in any kind of reality like we've done before. She talks loudly about being an "inmate" and feeling bad for what she did. I suppose she does feel as if she's in prison. Next thing, she says: "I was serenaded by a hundred homeless people last night" and then goes on to talk about the woman in the bed opposite her being a Jehovah's Witness involved in some kind of plot. Snaps angrily at us when we try to change the topic and insists that we should listen and believe her. She next tells us that she has been to the "chicken farm" and that she will be cooped up there for the rest of her life. I feel so exposed and embarrassed. Not only do I look as if I had the plague, but my Mum is also talking nonsense and getting angry at me when I don't agree with her. It's like being a teenager on steroids. It's surprising that I don't become delusional as well.

In an obviously desperate last attempt, my dad tries to refocus the conversation on something Mum could potentially become interested in. "Karen, what do you think of this one?" my dad interrupts. He shows Mum some potential prom dresses, and she looks intently at the phone screen. I know how much she actually does care, still, about me. But the topic would have been my last choice. How can he even think about my prom when I don't even feel up to going out to buy milk now? It annoys me anyway that he's begun trying to "crowdsource" opinions for my prom dress via WhatsApp. Mum doesn't really have an opinion on any of the dresses he shows her. I don't like them. I should be out shopping with her like my friends. Or just not go.

Dad actually sent back the crimson one I chose from a discount online shop. He claimed it looked "cheap" (well, it was actually cheap!) and that it was made from bad quality material: "You'll catch fire in that dress!". It's not as if I'm ever going to wear it after prom. Naturally the neckline plunges far too much for his liking, which is why the dress had to go back. I wish he could actually see that it was a wonder I even considered going to prom at all. I feel ugly and no longer laugh when Dad tries to be funny about ridiculous dress options that would cover me from head to toe or when he tries to show me pictures of really bad prom dresses to try to cheer me up. I just want prom, school and everything else to be over and done with as soon as possible. It would be great if I could at least have some control over wearing a prom dress I liked – however inappropriate it is. Mum advises me to avoid dresses with "slits everywhere" and to "Get a size 14" because of my age. I have no idea what that means, and we end up laughing about prom dresses, even though I hate thinking of a prom I don't really even want to go to in the first place.

There are losses and changes for anyone who has had a stroke and for anyone who loves that person. Most models of grief have something in them about the anger that follows such loss. My anger kind of went

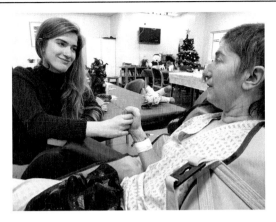

Figure 3.1. Karen and Tashi celebrating Christmas 2018

underground into some kind of passive aggressive version of it. I once read about these forests that burn underground and that was my anger – something eating away at things underground. It took so many different forms for me and makes better sense to me now that I've read up a little more about how people, teenagers and children specifically, struggle when a parent becomes ill or specifically when they have a brain injury.

It's strange to think of grief when someone is still alive. At least for a time. I suppose I was so busy trying to be what I thought I needed to be for my family, that it did not feel right to express anger in any other way.

Prepare for it and know it's going to be there. Recovery is not a simple process, and I was really surprised at the anger my mother sometimes expressed. I remember how difficult it was for all of us when we showed her the emotion icons on the aphasia app and she kept pressing the "Anger" face. At the time she did not have words and it was easy to think that she must be struggling to say how she really feels, but maybe she was just angry. I can see this now as her frustration at not being able to understand what is going on and then not being able to respond to what she finally understands is going on. The keyboard episode was really hard to take since we only wanted to be helpful to her and yet every suggestion just led to further frustration for Mum. How scary the world must have looked to Mum – seeing a keyboard that doesn't make sense to her, believing that she is in prison or subject of some experiment or plot. Yet it felt hard to take: The anger of someone you're trying to help. But it's very important – hard as this is – not to take it personally. Although, that was difficult: My mother was sometimes angry at me or my dad. Never at my little sister. She's less angry at me now, and more expressive of love and tolerance, but I suppose there was a lot I did at some point to be angry at.

There's also anger at the situation or the system. It seems so impersonal: At one point, we hardly ever saw a doctor. They seemed to always be so busy. But we were always there; so, where were they? We learned of their study days, research days and so on. So, it felt really difficult not to be angry sometimes: How can they be so busy that they're never actually with the patient they are supposed to be busy with? It is also really frustrating that the nurses are not allowed to discuss much with relatives – they have to defer to the doctors, who never really seem to be there anyway. This will remain a bit of a mystery for me, I'm afraid.

And even the simplest things can feel really triggering. When Mum's OT asked us to join in with Mum and make those cards with her, it really threw me. A lot is made of helping patients choose, but sometimes it feels – as a relative – as if you have much less choice. There's a whole back story to why I sometimes avoid doing art with other people. She had no way of knowing that I would tense up just thinking of doing art with my sister, who often could sometimes crumple up her drawings because she felt furious that they were not good enough. And that was how Mum felt too – she could not even put together a card. But then the anger and frustration circles around: Why make cards anyway? It's a bit like basket weaving – utterly pointless given that even Valentine's Day had passed. Mum would always tell me how important it is to find meaning, purpose and mastery in what you do. The card-making episode could not offer that. But it can be so hard to deal with the anger of someone who obviously begins to realise that they are struggling with stuff they could previously do. It scared me. I had some ideas of what we may all find more calming and positive, namely the "wet-on-wet" painting Mum did with me when she was home schooling me and training in Steiner Waldorf Education. But it seems so difficult for the system to accommodate anything like this, that I perhaps only mentioned it once to the OT instead of actually finding a way to do it with Mum.

Anger can also make you do things that seem self-destructive or hurtful to people who are trying to be kind or supportive. My dad once told me of a blind guy he saw outside a railway station. The man was standing on the edge of a busy street, almost lurching into traffic, evidently waiting for a taxi. When my dad asked him: "Are you alright?", he responded angrily: "Yeah, of course. What about you?". I think I was a bit like this and maybe it would have been good for me to talk with someone. It just felt impossible and unsafe to talk with a counsellor or teachers at school – it's too close to my normal for me to engage with it. But maybe I should have tried a bit more.

My anger at my dad came out in just dragging my feet, passively resisting the sense of urgency, the pressure to be a "good girl". It felt like our whole life had been reduced to hospital visits and parking lots, hospital beds. And there was a part of me that just wanted to resist this as much as possible. Look at your anger as well – it's normal. It's there. You can be forgiven for feeling it and you can also expect to experience it from your parents or others who're sharing the experience with you. I think it's important to find some outlet for it and my solitary walks and daydreaming, together with frequent infringements of house rules and so on, were part of how I expressed my anger.

I think it's important to feel what your anger is actually all about – what's underneath it. Maybe there's something unmet, an unmet need or something. For me, it had something to do with actually feeling as if I was suffocating in the house, in the situation, in my family. If you can pinpoint what the need is below all the anger, you can find a way out of it a bit more. No pressure. But like the heading of the chapter suggests: Anger is just one letter short of danger and maybe that's important to think about.

I found out that around 20% of adolescents who experienced a parent having a stroke, actually later undergo psychiatric admission at some point of their life. There is much to stress about, to be angry about, to go off the rails about when your parent is there but also not there, and your life is there, but also not there. I think it would have been good to feel more in control of something – even if it was a really badly chosen prom dress. That was my need for control. But then Dad probably had to feel that he was helping all of us be as "normal" as possible, so that he tried to compensate for Mum not being there to help me choose a prom dress. That was his need for control. The one thing my mum wanted us to do was to listen to her ravings, no matter how insane and out of control they were. That was her need for some control. I suppose we get angrier and angrier when we lose all sense of control. So that 20% psychiatric admission figure does not really surprise me at all, now that I think of it.

Chapter 4

Identity check

It's Easter holidays and I am at home with Léa. Dad could not take leave for the whole holiday, so I am playing the role of the dutiful daughter and don't really feel like going out with friends anyway. I've made a to do list with my sister in big pink and blue lettering: "Text about prom; Clean toilets; Clean landing area; Pack away clothes; Take plants downstairs; Get Léa dressed and ready; Do maths with Léa; Laundry (fold); Laundry (start); Sweep kitchen; House of art with Léa; Somba pills…". The list goes on. I wrote "To do for Me" in childish pink bubble letters. It's as if this is one role I could play – just losing myself in doing all these endless things I suppose Mum always did for us or Dad helped out with when he wasn't working. I think: "I never want children. Maybe I can donate my eggs or something" as I cross off some of the completed tasks, skipping the ones I know I'll never do.

We're trying to teach Mum how to use Siri on her phone to text us. She can't say the words clearly and laughs hysterically: "Text Tashi!" she repeats. I read

DOI: 10.4324/9781003171676-4

out what Siri thinks she said: "Text thirsty O God". An image of someone crawling in a desert pops into my head. It is good to hear Mum laughing out loud to this. My sister and Dad are also laughing. When we get home, it's as if my sister feels much better about the future. She makes plans: "I can clean my room so Mum can sleep with me". Later I see her at the kitchen table drawing plans and notes for the house. In big red letters she's written: "We can use a list for everyday and the stairs could be escylators if we cold not have a lyft".

Despite the good moments with Mum and the signs that she is making progress, I feel so stuck. I just want to do something, anything, which doesn't feel like that movie *Groundhog Day*. Or night more like. It feels like an endless night – like when we went to Iceland one year and the days seemed so short. I wake up with a weight on my chest. And, of course, I feel guilty for wanting change, excitement, diversion, when Mum and Dad are really struggling and there is the expectation for me to step up and be the ideal big sister for my little sister. I read a quote once of someone describing depression as feeling colour blind in a world where everyone keeps telling you how colourful it is. I'm not even sure I have depression – more just feeling like I'm going through the motions of life, as if I have no real sense of identity anymore. It doesn't feel as if I can have the luxury of having depression, or an identity. Things need doing, things need to get done. Things should have been done.

I sit surrounded by old photographs. I've scattered them everywhere, making a pile of the ones I want to keep. This is the product of going through hundreds of yellow Kodak film packets, taking out all the old pictures – most of them from before I was born. Most of them are of Mum. In one photo, she stands against a blue wall – it looks like a Greek island or somewhere sunny. There are some yellow roses in a flower box on a windowsill. Her eyes are closed and she's enjoying the last rays of the sun. She's wearing a short, floral dress and she smiles. There's a photo of her surrounded by broken branches on snow covered ground. Must be Canada, I think. There are some photos of my dad – his hair is longer than I've ever seen it and he told me once that the picture was taken somewhere in Central Park.

I know Dad won't like this – he can be sentimental at times and probably aims to put all the photos into an album or something, but I don't care. I doubt he'll have the time to actually do it. I can't help myself. I carefully tape these pictures, art prints, drawings I made, train tickets to every open inch of wall in my room. I feel like a spider spinning a web or a caterpillar spinning a cocoon. It takes ages to cover everything. It's as if each of these things is something tangible from a previous life of holidays, friends, family. When Dad comes up to my room, he begins to say: "I hope you didn't use blu-tack…" and then he gets lost in the pictures just like I did. He starts commenting on them and wonders with me about where some of the ones of Mum, before he had met her, were taken.

It's my birthday and we're having obligatory pancakes. I'm 16 today and feel much older. Dad has wrapped a Happy Birthday banner around my sister, who has to sing Happy Birthday to me as she pretends to be a "singing birthday card" like the actual card my grandmother sent her. We visit Mum today and I'm delighted to see that they've moved her into a single room. I stroke Mum's hair as she, Dad and my sister sing "Happy Birthday" to me. Mum got the room because Dad made a case that she's obviously being disturbed by being around other patients and that – in turn – some of the things that she believes and says could also be disturbing to other patients. It feels like an incredible luxury to shut the big red door of the room and not to hear the groans, snores or assorted beeps, alarms and noise of the ward. It says a lot that this feels like luxury.

But strangely, Mum has found the move away from the crowded ward confusing. She thought that she was being placed in a mortuary and said something about having given half her body to another woman. It makes sense really, since she has in fact lost contact with the left side of her body and obviously tries to understand what had become of it. We just want to be with her, calmly, but she goes on to tell a harrowing story of a man and woman who died to save the life of their child. The saddest thing Mum says is just before we go. In a moment of clarity, she pleads with us not to leave: "When you go, I lose track of who I am". We go home and I stare for a while at the young woman with blond hair crouching in a field of flowers. Does she know? One day she will be my mum and sing to me on my 16th birthday from a hospital bed, sometimes talking nonsense.

Dad visits her on his own a bit more often since I'm revising for my exams. He tells me after one of the visits that Mum explained to him that "Everything everyone says comes true". He agreed to test this with Mum and said to her: "OK then – you're a banana". And she responded: "Funny you should say that – earlier today I really was a banana and they cut me in half". Even though this was no joke really, and even though it had some sense to it (again, maybe something to do with perceiving only half her body), Mum is somehow able to laugh about these things a bit more now and there's less anger about feeling that we do not listen to her. Her team is also discussing longer-term rehabilitation options for her in places like Blackheath, Putney and so on. So, as it becomes Spring, there seems to be some progress – for Mum at least, even though she keeps thinking that she's "stuck in Le Havre". I remember the daytrip we did as a family to Le Havre during a camping holiday in France. After the quaint medieval villages we had seen, Le Havre was a shock: Inhospitable, grey, concrete, modernist. We could find only a small patch of green in this World Heritage concrete jumble and ended up having a picnic there, only later realising that we had been sitting among the dog turds. Being stuck in Le Havre really would be the worst possible thing for Mum and it's no surprise that this is where she now imagines she is.

Turning 16 should be something, but it just is not. I feel as if I really no longer know who I am. Actually, getting older does not seem like a good idea to me at all; just longer and more To Do lists like the ones I made in the Easter holidays. Those pictures and mementos on my bedroom walls do little to remind me of who I am or where I belong. Today is the day of my first GCSE exam. Have I revised? Vaguely, I've skimmed the subheadings of my textbook and drawn out a couple of plant diagrams. It's nowhere near enough but the exam is just Biology and I've managed to get A's for the last year with no revision. I know I shouldn't be thinking like this. It's so lazy and I hate myself for it, but I guess it's too late now. I pay attention in class at least – the teachers always say I "confuse them", because I love learning and get good grades, but the homework is few and far between. I think they're taken in by me. I feel like an imposter really. It takes little to convince them: Now and then asking a question in class. Never really indicating that I'm falling apart with my work. Basically, that's enough.

I feel my heartbeat in my neck as I stand in line waiting for my name to be called, I watch my classmates walk in – clutching pencils and rulers, their last defence against the education system. Finally, my name is called, mispronounced in every way. Is that even possible? I sit in the freezing exam hall staring at the paper in front of me, it stares back, challenging me. We are only allowed to start when they say so. For now, we have to listen to the woman at the front of the hall as she regurgitates the instructions: "If you are found cheating you will immediately be made to leave and will be disqualified from all exams". What about people who aren't caught? Lucky them, I guess. I don't even have the motivation to try to cheat, what happens will happen and if I get a bad grade, that's completely on me. On me. That's a phrase I never used before so much and now I do. It feels like there's a lot on me – my fault, my stuff. I suppose that this is actually appropriate: Becoming an adult seems to be the process of slowly taking more and more "on me".

The exam is a blur. It seems unimportant really. I finish the exam half an hour early – is that good? Bad? Can't blame them – it's on me. I check that I've actually done all the questions. I'd like to say I finished early, but it's because I knew everything and answered it easily but honestly, I just answered what I could and I'm hoping it's satisfactory enough. I spend my time waiting doodling on the back page: A huge eyeball. Nobody is allowed to leave the hall until all the time is up. "Have a nice day!" I write under the eyeball: The words look almost like a threat. I don't even know if my days are good or bad anymore, they just pass. I hope whoever is reading this has a better idea of how their day is going.

At lunch I get a call, it's my dad, I answer "Hi Dad – is everything OK?" He doesn't normally call me during the day, so I have no idea what it's about.

"Hey – just wanted to let you know they're moving Mum to Putney today, she's in the transport right now on her way." That's very good news, we've been waiting for this since Christmas, finally she's going to a place that is actually designed to help her with rehab. "That's great! Does that mean we are going to London this weekend?" I ask, I know I should probably spend the weekend revising but I'd much rather take a trip to London and realistically it's not like I'd accomplish much anyways. "Yes, but Tashi," I know what's about to come, "you have to stay on the ball, I want you to do at least three hours of revision every night this week." It sounds little – it's too much. I mumble something of an agreement and he hangs up.

I was stressed for the first couple of exams, and rightly so – they went fairly terribly – but after that I stopped caring really. The absolute worst that could happen is I don't get into my first choice sixth form, so what? At least I wouldn't have to access the "excellent pastoral care" available from that curvy corridor. Then I'll just go to my second, far less appealing, choice. I have a flashback to their open day: Chaos, sitting at a little table in a hall full of people also sitting at little tables talking to "advisors" who look a bit like parole officers or social workers and who obviously struggle to be there... A feeling as if you've not really left school, in contrast with the other choice. Yes, it would be horrible if my second choice was my only choice. Mum went to Newnham College in Cambridge and she always made me understand just how important it is for "young women" to make the most of the opportunities they now have, since these were so hard won. My birthday copy of Malala's autobiography remains carefully unread. What would she think of me now?

I'm in trouble. The drawing of the eyeball and "Have a nice day!" got enough attention for the Vice Principal to call my dad to discuss "concerns" about my wellbeing. Now, if I had tattooed that eyeball onto myself or graffitied my message over the Vice Principal's car, that would be worrying. I listen while the Vice Principal and my dad discuss me. I speak only when I need to: Yes, I'll think about whether I'm OK and whether I want to see the counsellor or go to Centre 33 or whatever – anything they think would help (not). I resist the urge to joke about being glad that they have their eye on me or seeing eyeball to eyeball. After the call, my dad seems conflicted with himself as he half agrees with me that a doodle and a message scrawled on an exam paper are perhaps not the clearest signals of being mentally unwell, con-sidering what we've experienced in the hospital.

Dad shows me and my sister a video of Mum in a music therapy session. She is singing a song that she wrote with a music therapist and there's also a photo of the lyrics. Mum played piano before the stroke and got up to grade 8 or something when she was still young. In the video, she only plays with her right hand while the therapist fills in the bass notes. Mum sings in the video:

My name is Léa
I live in the top floor
And I go with my cars
Broom broom in the hallway
My name is Léa
I have my own secret den

And sometimes there's a castle
With a secret door
That leads to a fairy
My name is Léa
I am tall with blonde pony tails
My sister is Tashi
I like breakfast in the car
On the way to school
Guava, papaw, raspberries
Blueberries – delicious to eat
In my den
My sister is Tashi
She is 14 going on 16
And she likes to play her guitar
She would fly away in an aeroplane
If she could be a pilot
Pieter makes us food
He makes us laugh and laugh and laugh and laugh
And then we eat it all up
And laugh some more

The words are simple, and the song is halting, but we are all deeply touched by it. Mum's still in there – and so much of her. And we are not with her and that is all she wants: To be home. The song shows through all the cracked notes that she holds us inside of her, even if I sometimes don't know who I am. Even if she gets my age wrong – more like 16 going on 21, but I would fly away in an aeroplane if I could be a pilot. I can't remember when last I played my guitar or made up any songs myself.

We are walking to the train station, our little family, my sister swinging happily between my dad and I, we are on our way to see my mum in London for the first time. I'm excited, largely for the change in scenery but also because we've already been there before and now, we will actually see whether it lives up to our expectations. The first time we visited, Mum was still in hospital, and we had to meet with her team in a powder-blue boardroom around a huge table, to talk about our expectations for Mum's rehab. It felt a lot like visiting my first-choice college.

But it takes us nearly three hours to get to the place. As at our first visit, I am struck by the shabby, stately home feel, although it is also as if the money suddenly ran out for this stately home. The ceilings are high and there's something cool and edgy about the place too, a bit like an art school or something. There's even a bust of Charles Dickens somewhere – evidently, he had something to do with it. And a grand piano in a ballroom with parquet flooring. It feels so different from the narrow linoleum corridors of the hospital in which Mum has been confined.

We walk past an art studio stuffed with artworks and inspiration on the walls. We walk past a lady in a wheelchair holding a collection box for the place. She's the same person on a poster of the Royal Hospital for Neuro-disability – Putney – to call it by its full name. She must have been here forever. She sits quietly smiling, holding her collection box. I wonder if this is Mum's fate as well. She reminds me a little of those Chinese lucky cats that gently wave their paws up and down, bestowing good luck and happiness on you.

We walk past a section with toys for children – it seems incredible. There are well-cared-for plants in pots, a television, toys. Comfortable. Family oriented. Homey. We're struck by the difference from the hospital. Before Mum's admission, Dad had to complete a massive questionnaire about her — all her likes, dislikes, interests and so on. It took much longer to complete than the communication questionnaire we previously completed for her. I never knew he knew her that well. I wonder what he would put down for me on a similar questionnaire. I wouldn't even be able to answer it for myself.

We are led to my mum's ward, it's a new extension to the hospital, a clean modern design – nothing like the smelly, faded hospital cubicles we got to know so well. Mum's room is very light with a window overlooking a small forest, she has her own TV and a CD player. "Mum, this place looks great – do you like it here?" I ask, "It's good, yeah." She replies simply. "Have you had any physiotherapy yet?" My dad asks, she nods "Yes. And I did crafts too". I smile, I'm glad to see this place is already making an effort. "But when am I coming home?" She asks, looking at us with sad eyes. She asks this again and again in the conversation. It's hard to explain to her that she can't right now – the house is only just habitable for us let alone her and especially since she is going to need full-time carers, if there is funding for this. Let alone the fact that she's here to access rehab which she would be so unlikely to get once she's back home.

"Well, Karen, see there are a lot of things we need to do first, we need to completely strip and paint all the walls and fix up the garden and sort out the guest room upstairs, and you are not going to be able to use a stair lift so we will either have to convert the downstairs into a bedroom and bathroom for you or build a whole new extension in the garden." My dad tries to sound soothing but I can tell he's stressed just talking about everything that we need to do. That is, if Mum is ever well enough to come home. "Why don't you do that? I want to come home!" I suppose it's valid, but she doesn't understand how difficult it actually is: "Mum, Dad has to work every day, and even then, if he was working round the clock, it would still take time" I explain, she looks rejected and irritated: "Pay someone to do it for you." She's sounding angry now. "I don't have the money!" my dad laughs, "God, I wish it were that simple. I miss having you on my team though, you were so good at painting in our old house – remember?" Distraction still works. She smiles "Yes. I can help you now." My dad and I share a glance, I don't think she realises how impaired she really is.

We change the topic – instead talking about my GCSEs, not much better. I say yes, I have been revising, yes, of course I'm on top of it, yes, they are going really well. I know none of this is really true, but I don't want to have one deal with my dad getting angry or making my mum stressed for me. So, I answer the questions as simply as possible, trying to at least not make the situation any worse.

When Mum loses interest, she suddenly says: "I have 7000 arms". What on earth does this mean? At least she's no longer thinking that the staff are killing her. Dad explores this with her: "Can you show me your arms?". She shows her right arm, and then tries to reach over to her left arm and becomes vague. After the nurses come in to attend to Mum, Dad and I make our way to the cafeteria, picking up my little sister, who has been spending time with another little girl whose dad had a stroke as well. She's happily sitting on an oversized dog, while the other girl is amusing herself with some soft toys.

"Neglect… Mum's not aware of things on her left side." My dad tries to explain why my mum does not notice things on her left side and it makes more sense, for a moment. But it's hard to hold in mind when you're with her. He reminds me of the mirror box they tried previously without much success; a way of "tricking" the mind into processing things correctly on the side of the body that is being "neglected". My dad had explained something about this to me before; often people with strokes lose the ability to move a side of their body, and sometimes this means that their brains are completely unaware of that side. So, as he explained it to me, my mum can only really see the right side of her vision – the left doesn't really exist for her. The same is true for her awareness of her body. It doesn't just affect vision, it means that she could logically know there is an arm on her left side but she has no idea of how to move it or where it is, although she could sometimes be made aware of it for a moment. We try to help her become aware of her left side by moving her right hand to touch her left – my dad says it perhaps feels like when you get a dead arm and you have that weird alien sensation, you know it's your arm logically but you can't feel or move it.

When we get back to Mum, I try to ask her more about her arm. She explains: "Only one of them works". I wonder what she thinks the other 6999 arms are for, but I don't want to upset her. My sister touches Mum's right hand, then her left, "I can only see two" she says in a matter-of-fact way. Mum seems to shrug. We play around with the idea – what if she really did have 7000? "Mummy would be an octo-pus!" my sister says, giggling at the thought. "And Mummy would be really good at helping with paint-ing the house," I add. Fortunately, the nurses come to change Mum, as we can see that she has become tired and irritable. I can't imagine how it must feel to have to wait for others to change you.

Mum has been in Putney now for some months. We have made many trips there and back and sometimes we dip into London on our way back home, perhaps stopping over for a pizza or trying to pop into a museum before or after visiting, so that we at least have something to tell Mum the next time we see her. We leave at dawn and usually sleep on the train back. Weekends become the same kind of blur as weekdays and sometimes I am so tired on my way there or back, that I sleep or mindlessly listen to music some seats away from my dad and sister. I observe our little routines, like stopping at the little kiosk at Putney station to get Biltong (South African "jerky") or "Beskuit" (South African rusks). Sometimes Dad is really annoyed at how I dress – too revealing in his opinion, especially in that one blouse which he keeps wanting to bin or shrink to nothing in the wash. On the Tube, I travel apart from my dad and sister and notice the gaze of strangers, appraising me. I sometimes imagine that I am just commuting to London – not travelling to a hospital. That I am older and that anything is possible.

Today, we are surprised to be met by Mum's occupational therapist, who seems delighted to meet us. We can only visit over weekends and holidays, so it's really special to be able to meet with one of Mum's team over the weekend. She has a paper parcel and holds it out – one for me and one for Léa. We carefully unwrap our parcels, because the OT has told us that they contain something fragile. Mum has made me a little heart shaped clay box in salmon, with a green T (for my name) on top of its lid. My sister gets a blue, multicolour clay rainbow that seems able to hold a candle at each end. I thank Mum for my gift with a hug. She says: "It's got a snake on top... You're a snake". I'm not sure what she means by this – maybe the hiss of a "shi" in my name, but gloss over it, even if my guilty conscience makes me wonder what else she could mean. Clearly my sister is a rainbow or ray of light or something... I wish my conscience were clearer as I hold this simple, honest, and somehow beautiful little gift.

I've finished my exams. I will only find out my grades in August. I don't know if the waiting makes it better or worse really… Next week I'm going to Germany for the first time, on my own. I'm going to be visiting a family introduced to us by a German family friend. It feels like my dad is making an effort to do *something* for – or is it about – me. Things are strained at home and he doesn't understand why I keep not making more of an effort with things. It's as if he wants me to be one of those smiling girls on YouTube explaining how they managed to turn their parent's illness into some kind of motivation for them: *I did this for you, Mum*. I don't seem to have the energy to do this. I look forward to the new experience and the freedom of travelling abroad on my own. Maybe I can prove something – what?

Today, I am going to London on my own. My uncle has come over from Canada and he is staying over in Putney to be closer to Mum. Dad is desperately working on the house – for what? We're not even sure anymore if we can continue to stay here or if the house is ever going to be suitable for Mum. Evidently, it would be too expensive to adapt. I sit, slouched against my seat with earphones in. I am aware that I look like the typical teenager. No one would imagine that I'm heading to London to be with my mum who just happens to be in a neurorehabilitation hospital. Suddenly my phone rings. I check: It's my dad: "Tashi, Mum's been moved, she's in St Georges' Hospital now - she's in intensive care". I am stunned, not sure if I understood. Is this some kind of test or something? "God, why?" I ask.

"She has a chest infection, they moved her last night, apparently. They haven't said how serious it is but…" he trails off.

"OK so what do I do – I'm already on the train? Am I allowed to see her?".

"I think you should meet your uncle like we planned then go to St Georges' Hospital together – is that OK?". He seems to be thinking aloud, not sure of what would be allowed or not. It feels like that call I made when Mum first had her stroke.

"Yes, OK I'll do that." I don't even know where St Georges' Hospital is… My whole attention is now on conserving the battery of my phone, making sure it's charged as much as I can charge it, because I'm on my own and will need to find my own way there. It scares me. But I actually begin to enjoy the challenge of finding my way – it takes my mind off things. After an hour, I get to St Georges' Hospital.

My uncle is waiting for me at the entrance. Imagine – all the way from Canada and we find one another here. It's been two years since I saw him last, and he hasn't changed a bit. I feel so happy to see a familiar face. Hugs, smiles.

"Hi! How are you? Have you seen my mum?".

He smiles, "I'm OK, just got in last night – I've been with your mum all this morning but she's under a lot of medication so she's asleep. The doctors say she's stable, they're being extra cautious because she's in a high-risk category."

He leads me to the room she's staying in; we have to sanitise our hands before we go in. Seeing her in bed like this reminds me of when she was back in Addenbrooke's, she looks so small, vulnerable. I hold her hand: "Hey Mum, I'm here" she groans slightly; I think she squeezes my hand – I would like to think that she does.

My uncle and I stay with her until visiting time is over, we're both so tired by the end we go straight back to our rooms back at the hospital. It's shabby, but cheap. They're just about to refurbish it or something, but at this moment, it seems to have the ghosts of the past in the form of so many carpet stains, cigarette burns....

I lie in bed thinking about how I did not visit Mum last week. At the time, I decided not to go along with Dad and Léa. I can't even remember why. Maybe I just wanted the house to myself; maybe I was tired... I feel selfish and stupid: What if she dies now? At least I'm here now, but I should have gone last week as well... After grabbing a coffee along our way, we visit Mum the next day. It's so much more comfortable travelling with my uncle to the hospital this time. When we get to Mum's ward, a friendly nurse tells us the good news: Mum has just woken up.

"That's amazing!" exclaims my uncle, this is the first time he will be able to talk to her since the stroke.

"Karen, are you awake?". He asks tentatively, her eyes open slowly and I see the trace of a smile on her lips: "Hi Mum, I'm here too, do you know where you are?"

She struggles to say anything.

"You're in St George's Hospital, you have a lung infection and you were having trouble breathing." I try to sound calm but it's hard to see her like how she was shortly after the stroke. That night, my uncle and I are exhausted again, but we end up having pasta in a little Italian restaurant. I carefully try to avoid too much directed questioning about my plans for the future; how school is and so on. There are so many ways of deflecting and sounding cheerful and I know quite a few of them. Fake it till you make it. Or just fake it. I steer the conversation to Germany and my visit there. It seems silly, but at least it's safe ground.

I return home late. It was good to have the freedom of being in London. But it's a long walk back home. Things keep churning through my head. A trainee doctor told us that Mum should be discharged back to Putney tomorrow if all goes well. If all goes well. There's something so fragile about her; about us now. There's no guarantee. To me, it feels like bad things can and will happen all the time now. There are thoughts that flicker just on the edges of my awareness – like: "Will I ever be with her like before? Will she ever laugh like she used to? Will she ever…". I keep these thoughts on the edges of my mind, since thinking too much of any of these things just make me feel heavy and hopeless. It feels like we have to filter everything now, especially when we talk to Mum. I wonder how she feels about herself, about us now. Slowly, it feels like the string that attached her to our world is loosening, fraying. My dad says that we are her only anchor to our world, and I feel this too... But I am a very poor anchor – I feel as if I'm drifting most of the time too and as if there's very little anchoring me to the life I once had before Mum's stroke.

My dad once explained to me that depression is sometimes considered to be a form of learned help-lessness, referring to animal models where they throw rats in water. After some kind of experimental manip-ulation, some rats simply give up. What's the point? They must be thinking in their little rat brains.

Figure 4.1. Karen, Tashi and Léa playing piano in Putney

Figure 4.2. Karen and Somba in the hospital garden

I certainly felt like a rat. I felt helpless, hopeless, much of the time. There was this one visit, where Mum was having a hard time and being really difficult with staff and everyone around her. Léa was up and over and under Mum's bed, which made the whole situation feel even crazier. Somewhere an alarm was buzzing. I just sat in a corner and cried with laughter while my dad tried to keep some sense of order in the situation. I felt stuck and as if nothing ever really changed or improved and even if it did, some new disaster was just around the corner. Looking back now, it is clear just how far Mum has come. But in the situation, it seems as if every change, even good ones, bring new challenges that seem almost impossible to overcome.

This is how it felt when Mum suddenly got hospitalised again. She seemed so close to death and then somehow, she made a miraculous recovery. My advice to anyone in this situation would be to be really careful about managing hopes and expectations. My dad told me about the parable of the Chinese farmer, retold by Alan Watts. It is a story of a farmer, whose horse runs away after which his neighbours commiserate with him, telling him that he has had great misfortune. The farmer just responds with: "Maybe". When the horse returns the next day with some wild horses, the villagers visit the farmer and exclaim how lucky the farmer is. He again just responds with: "Maybe". His son then injures himself when he tries to break in one of the horses the next day and – you guessed it – the neighbours come along, expressing how unfortunate the farmer is. He just responds with: "Maybe". And so the story goes: The son is not drafted into the army the next day because of his injury – Yeah! "Maybe". And I wonder whether the story would just go on like this forever. An infinity of small or bigger ups and downs with the farmer's inevitable: "Maybe" suggesting a more stoical way of life.

We were like those villagers. When Mum gave me that little heart shaped box, I felt delighted that she had made something, but at the same time, fear and anxiety tinged the experience: Will this be it? What is

Mum going to be capable of? Eventually this was replaced with a simple acceptance of her generosity and her love and her kindness. When you look closely, there is always something of the person shining through their injury. This is something that gave me hope.

When you keep hoping for more, or for something very specific, that's dangerous and that's where the learned helplessness comes in. If I could go back in time and give myself advice, it would be not to think too much in the situation, but just to look for every sign of Mum just being Mum. As much or as little as that was possible at different times. That's real. When we get caught up in those worries and hopes, we are like those villagers in the. I once read a short quote: "No expectations… just gratitude" and that summarised something of a turning point for me. Things started feeling a little better when I stopped expecting things from Mum, or myself, or Dad… and when I could just feel simply grateful for things. I even tried keeping a gratitude journal in which I wrote down things I felt grateful for. I did not keep this up for long, but the idea stuck. Try it if you like, of course without expecting too much from yourself or from it.

Chapter 5

That's where the light gets in…

It is the strangest of times. We're sitting behind a plexiglass screen and trying to make ourselves understood – on both sides of the screen. They've rigged up a kind of baby monitor or something and we can just about hear one another. But what do we have to say? It's so difficult. Mum is sitting on the other side of the glass in a little room. My sister squirms uncomfortably on her chair. When we visited Mum before in this place, no longer Putney now, we have had to wear latex gloves, aprons, face masks. It's hard for my sister not to be bothered by these things. She tugs at the sweaty, oversized latex gloves. My mum wears a visor that mostly sits askew on her head. But it is still good to meet her in person, despite these COVID-19 measures.

Since March, we've had it all: First no visits, only connecting to FaceTime. Invariably frustrating for Mum, who ends up pressing her call button only a short while after our calls start. Once I asked her why she called for her carers so often, wondering if she should not perhaps try to deal with something herself

DOI: 10.4324/9781003171676-5

first. She said that she called them because she felt lonely. That made me feel sad. As lockdown lifted, we kept on hearing more and more stories of how people have been separated from their loved ones by COVID-19. Care homes, where people are not allowed to visit at all. Slowly, FaceTime gave way to seeing Mum in person, but always outside. Sometimes sitting what felt like next to a busy road in a little garden – the perfect metaphor for our family really. Is that my oasis? I thought wryly at the time, thinking back to that picture on the wall of Addenbrooke's.

If, two years ago, I saw myself sitting like this, on one side of a plexiglass divider, trying to make conversation with Mum, I would not have believed that this could be real. But here I am. I have brought along a friend's ukulele and I strum some chords on it. Mum beams at me. She smiles from ear to ear as I play something – anything. It brings to mind all those times when I was just strumming my guitar in my room instead of doing anything more constructive. There is so much history that leads up to this point.

Dad told me that he requested Mum's medical records and scans for her. When he explored the USB drive and CD that was sent by the hospital, he found that her medical records alone numbered more than 13,000 pages. These are only the records from Addenbrooke's Hospital and we have no records yet of her time in Putney or in the care home where she stays now. Just in the first five months after her stroke, she had fourteen brain scans (angiograms, CT-scans, one MRI-scan) and four chest X-rays – all on different occasions, tracking her progress or deterioration. It is possible to navigate through the scans on the CD and to see how the area affected by the stroke grows in size and then fades as you "slice" through the images. It is possible too, to see how there was first just an injured brain with almost no ventricles visible due to swelling. Then the images show a brain with the subsequent traces of "plumbing" aimed at relieving pressure: "burr holes", EVDs and eventually a shunt.

How can anyone summarise this history? There is the terse little report on the MRI-scan report which sums up the damage inflicted by the stroke, like a pessimistic school report:

MRI Report: Comparison to previous CTs from Nov 2018.

Haemorrhage in the right posterior mid brain and thalamus has decreased in size to a focal area of volume loss lined by hypointensity on T2, likely to be chronic blood product. There are no particular features to suggest an underlying midbrain cavernoma although this is not excluded. There is focal hyperintensity on T2 and FLAIR in right parietal white matter which is nonspecific and probably of long standing. There is haemosiderin staining on swan on the surface of the medulla, in the left occipital horn and along the path of a previous left posterior ventricular catheter. Focal high intensity on T2 and FLAIR on the left of the medulla is likely to be hypertrophic olivary degeneration. The ventricles are within normal limits in size with a right frontal ventricular catheter. No vascular abnormality on MRA.

I wonder, if someone could write a report on me, what it would say right now. What has improved? What has degenerated? Where did things go wrong? As I look back at this account of my mum's stroke and my experience of it, I see so many cracks – so many things I've left out. If this were a photo album, I would have whole episodes that I've not mentioned – pages stuck together in the book of memory.

There was the time I spent in Germany with that family I mentioned earlier on. It was a different world: Cycling through Berlin … feeling so far away from everything…. I actually felt happy there for the first time in a long while. Not understanding much German isolated me from the people around me – there were no real demands or expectations.

If this were an album, there would be a photo of the time we saw a live performance at the top of Arthur's seat when we went to Edinburgh for my sister's sixth birthday. It started raining but the band played on in the wind and rain and I felt as if I never wanted them to stop. I felt myself dissolve into the rain, the music and the landscape, forgetting everything that we would eventually have to deal with and do once we come down from the mountain.

Another photo in my timeline would be of me standing still in front of a group of deer at Richmond Park. A fawn looks inquisitively at me. Time stands still in this encounter, and I forget that we have just said bye to Mum; I forget that we are in Putney and still have another three hours of travelling back home. I forget about school, friends, relationships. All the stress of the preceding visit has drained away. It is exactly a year after Mum's stroke and we were allowed to take Mum for a first outing to Richmond Park. She had to travel separately in a special van and her driver and Occupational Therapist waited for her in the car park while we had an hour to visit with Mum. Mum was cold and uncomfortable and she was afraid that we would be too far away from the occupational therapist. She seemed frightened as we carefully pushed her wheelchair around and around on the accessible path, avoiding the café which she felt she could not tolerate because she was too embarrassed about how she looked. Dad asked her how she feels a year on from her stroke and she said: "I am awake and thinking about everything, but I am inside of myself fine, but outside not". For me, it's the opposite. But in the encounter with the deer, I feel like myself again.

There's a trip to Paris with my boyfriend, complete with selfies done retro style so we look like the students in the May '68 student revolution – all the more realistic with my brown corduroy fur-trimmed jacket with its torn pockets, barely holding in my lighters and cigarettes. In one picture I am sitting on his shoulders and there is just laughter – the world looks different when you sit on someone else's shoulders. I look back at these things and think: Am I vain? Selfish? An escape artist? I'm not sure. Maybe it's too early to judge.

There are many things I would not have photos of in my album, even if they claim to be part of my life. Why should I remember "results" day? Why should I hold onto interminable lessons at college? It is also sometimes too painful to think at all about how things were before Mum's stroke.

Yes, there are many cracks in this story and the cracks remind me of kintsugi – my dad pointed it out to me in the Fitzwilliam Museum and I became really interested in it. Look it up: "The Japanese art of putting broken pottery pieces back together with gold – built on the idea that in embracing flaws and imperfections, you can create an even stronger, more beautiful piece of art". I was intrigued by this idea ever since I heard of it. But the idea is still vague in my mind – I don't quite yet feel it: Our family does have these cracks running through it. So do I, Mum, Dad – all of us. One day, maybe, we'll be able to accept the cracks in ourselves and in our story a little more, so that we see things for however beautiful and however ordinary they are.

A concept which has really helped me in coming to terms (as far as that's possible) with Mum's stroke and this situation, has been ambiguous loss. *Pauline Boss (2000) described such loss in her book:* Ambiguous loss: Learning to cope with unresolved grief. *It turns out that this is a more helpful way of looking at the experience of brain injury from the point of view of a family, perhaps. Ambiguous loss is loss that occurs without closure or clear understanding; often it results*

Figure 5.1. Léa and Tashi visiting Karen during the COVID-19 pandemic

Figure 5.2. Tashi during the Edinburgh festival

in unresolved grief. When your parent has an illness or brain injury that changes everything, it can be very difficult to even allow yourself to feel a sense of loss. After all: They have not died. After all: You're OK and have so much to be thankful for. After all…

But that doesn't change the reality of the sense of loss that you have – every step of the way. It is a really weird thing to say, but in the initial phase, when your parent is unconscious perhaps, everything seems possible. It's like a dream from which they will probably wake up and talk and speak. But they don't always. Then there's the hope of rehab: They may not walk perfectly, but just hold on and maybe… But there's also the day the rehab team tells you they can't identify any more active goals for rehab and that they will be stopping "active" rehabilitation. And, yes, the person is with you still, but when they snap at you angrily or do something towards you that is out of character and clearly due to their injury, it is so difficult to feel the simple happiness you would like to feel in the situation. It is a little like losing them a little more, losing a little more hope, every now and then…

And wrapped up in this is also guilt: I want to love and accept them and be there for them, but they're different and sometimes I don't even know how and what I feel towards them. It is really OK to experience this ambiguity from time to time and if you can find a way of just letting it be, it does get better. I found it important not to try to be who I am not. Sure, I made things impossible for my dad and my family at times. Sure, there were times when I could have done better.

But that's me. And the same is true for all of us. We're in the same boat.

When a parent dies, I imagine, it's not simple of course. But you have an ending and the simple memories of the good times. With someone who has had a brain injury, it's a breath-holder through those times when the person seems not at all like themselves and you're left wondering whether things would get even worse. We have been lucky that Mum has recovered some of the very important qualities that make her who she is. Sometimes it's a gesture; sometimes it's her just being so kind or saying: "Thank you" all the time. Although her speech therapist once said it's just a filler (she also says "sorry" a lot), I can't think of a better filler than being thankful. And that is something she is teaching me. Whenever we have a good visit, we are thankful. Whenever we have a difficult visit, we can still be thankful for something; even if it's just the McDonalds Happy Meal that gets my sister's full attention on the way home.

I've not said anything yet about my spider plants. I can't help it: People give me spider plants when they hear that I have a number of them already. My bedroom is so small, but these plants fill every remaining space. Sometimes I bump into them and their water spills out. Other times, I forget to water them. They go on. And so do I. I think it's important for you to know that you can survive something bad happening to you or to someone you love too. I don't always like how I survived, or how I keep struggling with issues like who I really am or what I really want. And I go on – just like those spider plants in my room.

I still don't like the sound of the word acceptance *which reminds me of giving in or something, even if that's not what it means. Thankfulness also still sounds weird to me. But it is possible to live these things a little more as you care for or experience your parent in the different settings they'll be in and the different stages of their recovery. You must try not to wish your life or the moment away as you may do at times, because we don't ever know what's going to happen in the next moment.*

My sister makes the most beautiful drawings of our family. In one, Mum stands in the middle, with some blue bird (of happiness?) hovering over us. There are many purple hearts and my dad's hair is on end as if he's had shock treatment. It is a surprisingly happy picture that makes all of us smile every time we see it. Above the bird there's the word: Family. Often, I don't understand what we've been through or where we'll be going. I don't understand my sister's picture fully, or my dog's capacity for happiness. And it reminds me of a quote I saw: Don't try to understand everything, because sometimes it is not meant to be understood, but to be accepted. That word – acceptance – again.

There will be so much that you and your family don't understand and at first don't accept, but if you hang in there without being too critical of yourself; without lashing out too much at people around you; without hoping for too much and then feeling disappointed, maybe there is some degree of acceptance for you and your family too. Some things can't be mended, even with kintsugi. That's where the light gets in.

Chapter 6

What in my life is consistent?

I go through the house looking for photos of Mum, journals, notebooks. I find a little jar which Mum and Dad made just after I was born, with little strips of paper in it – each a wish for the future: Buy our own house… Get a dog… After unfurling the little bits of paper, I roll them up again and place them back in the jar. I wonder whether Mum and Dad will ever add any other strips of paper to the jar.

I find a blue A4 notebook in which she started, in typical Mum fashion, to keep a journal but discontinued it after a page or two. What she wrote here, more than a decade ago, touches me deeply as it is my story also:

> What in my life is consistent? If I could answer this, would I be closer to writing out my values? There has been a lot of change – too many changes – and now another one. A new place to live, a new part of the country, a new house, a new school, a new job for Pieter. It makes me think of things that make me happy. What will

DOI: 10.4324/9781003171676-6

make this big move work? I think the stable part of life is way down the road in time, that I am still a 20-something with few attachments or responsibilities; a great future and ample opportunities. However; that is not where I should be at in my thinking. So, to start with, my list of things or ways that I am consistent:

- Still diabetic (24 years).
- Always think the best of people.
- Have always been happy with where I am… although I think that is because I have always been assuming that maturity / stability / comfort is yet to come (is this the "I am still 20-something" factor?).
- I form respectful and meaningful friendships with lots of talking at the core.
- I love learning new things.
- I don't want to damage the earth.
- I have always liked to plan out ideas.
- I am focused when I work; I work fairly hard when I work.
- I am strong physically.
- I love my family – I have always loved and looked up to my family whether my first family or my current young family.
- I really like being with Pieter; this has never changed. I always look forward to seeing him and enjoy talking with him. If / when I am frustrated, I consistently bounce back. I keep liking him: It just doesn't change! This surprises me, because in the past – after a

while – I needed to move on. That has never happened with Pieter. I know I get frustrated and "hurt" and all sorts of emotions tumble out at difficult times, but it doesn't make me stop loving him.

- I have loved Tashi from before she was born – every day of her life. I am consistent in my love for her. I am consistently awed by her. I am always interested in her, in being with her. I want to care well for her, to listen to her needs and match them. I want to be more available to do things with her. I hope when we move we can do some nice projects together. I hope we have more time.

- I am sentimental, I think about people that are no longer in my life, especially my Dad. I am deeply affected by death, even of people I don't know. I miss my dad so much and feel undone by his death. Something that I always thought was consistent – my Dad – turned out not to be. I thought he would always be around or at least that I would be settled by the time I no longer needed him so much.

This has been my account of what happened. Mum's own story, in her own words, has not yet been heard. Mum finds writing and reading very difficult now. This is what she says when asked about her experience, and in it, I find that consistency she was looking for more than a decade ago – something I do not yet have:

My life was changed in 2018 when I had a stroke. I can remember things that happened yesterday and a while ago, but I don't remember much after the stroke. The stroke affected me in many ways. I am dizzy and feel very hot or cold. I need a carer to come and help me with everything. I can't use anything on my left side – leg, arm… My eyes have changed too. I see out of my right eye only and my left eye feels like I have a mask on. And my voice is different – I can't speak out of my left side and my voice is different – dysarthric. It means I don't speak very clearly. It feels like I can

Figure 6.1. Tashi's painting of the little ceramic heart-shaped box Karen gave her

Figure 6.2. A family visit to Richmond Park

only hear out of my right side – I can't hear anything with my left ear.

My memory is very patchy for the early days after the stroke. I remember using my thumb to give a thumbs up to people, but maybe that's just because I learned that I did this. I remember a friend of mine coming to Addenbrooke's. She's someone I know from Cambridge where I went to university and she is from Canada. I can remember her visiting me in hospital. She had her hair coloured and I said something about it and we laughed a lot. I haven't seen her in a long time, but I saw her a lot in Putney. I remember the girls and Pieter visiting me. I remember my youngest daughter playing with people in the garden. I also remember that I wanted her to go to the bathroom before going back home – it was a long way back home from where I was in rehab.

I remember having strange thoughts after the stroke and they felt real to me at the time. Now I see them as dreams. These are the stories I remember: I remember thinking that I was a captain of a ship – that was when I was in hospital. There were a lot of people around me and at the time I was not sure how to be a good captain. I also remember a yellow house and a big farm, a friend's country home and I remember looking after her father's first wife. I was very worried about what I would do for a living: I thought I could look after a mad woman or something. I remember when I was at Putney I had a dream that I was with my brother, trying to go to a hospital in Canada. I remember thinking that I had 7000 hands. Now I feel I have a phantom arm that no one can see, but when I was in Putney, I think people told me to have a funeral for my phantom arm. All these things seem much clearer to me than life in the hospital and in rehab. Maybe I had these dreams because I was bored.

I remember my life before the stroke clearly. My youngest daughter, Léa, used to say that I have a Mummy smell and she used to sniff my neck. One of my best memories is going to the Cheetah Sanctuary in South Africa and our whole family stroking the cheetah – the one we have a photo of. The cheetahs loved Léa and she loved them, and this is why I made *her a cheetah suit when she was a bit older. I also remember her baptism and how she tried to doctor one of our friends who was very ill with cancer. I was embarrassed but also laughed a lot when she asked whether a great aunt was a clown, because she had too much makeup on. That's Léa – she says what she thinks like kids do when they're little. I remember her first birthday when we were camping in France. She was turning one and I was very proud of her. We didn't have much space in the car and forgot some things, so I ended up making bunting in the car from some paper and string I found. We were in a camp ground and I remember putting the bunting up and Tashi made her a cake. It felt like a really special birthday.*

I remember that Tashi was born prematurely, and I remember that I was her teacher for two years when I home schooled her. I loved Tashi so much and when I had another baby, I worried that I would never be able to love another child as much as I loved Tashi. I remember a lot of what Tashi did when she was little. I remember that I used to do maths with her by bouncing a ball and asking her to do her multiplication tables and she knew it by the end of it. Some of my happiest memories are about taking Tashi to Canada and South Africa. I loved introducing her to the snow and hoped that she would enjoy it as much as I did. I wanted to show her how big and good the world is. I think that my stroke had a big impact on Tashi in her GCSEs and A-levels. I don't think she got as much attention as she needed – we had a little girl, and I was unwell after my stroke. I think she really missed me at a time when she needed me to be there for her. The last years at school can be hard. I missed meeting her first really serious boyfriend and I was very embarrassed about having her friends see me – because of how I look. I was never embarrassed about my husband and my girls seeing me, because they were good to me, but I was very worried about anyone else seeing me, because I wasn't as good as normal. I am worried that it was hard for Tashi as well – and that it was embarrassing for her that I had these problems.

Covid changed things for the worse: I am very lonely and not allowed to see visitors as easily as before. My husband and youngest daughter come to see me over the weekends, but they need to do lateral flow tests and they have to wear gloves, masks, aprons… I miss having more visitors. I used to go to the doctor and now I have a nurse wearing a mask and there are lots of worries now about Covid. The only times I get to go out – and that is on my own with carers taking me – is to the hospital for appointments. I used to have to isolate in the past after these appointments, which meant that I was even more lonely.

I do less exercise now, during Covid. I feel sometimes I am a lost cause and that's why I get no physio now. They put me in an exercise class with old people and one physio: We do silly things like children's games and I can't even do it, because I am dizzy. I feel like I am really bad at everything. There are 90-year-olds who are better than me, because I can't speak well and I am dizzy all the time. I also get tired very quickly. Sometimes I think that this is not real – that this did not happen to me. Movies, books and dreams can feel more real than my life. Then it helps to talk to my husband and my family – I can check in with them that this is really happening and that I really had a stroke and that this is now my life.

The things I enjoy most are listening to audiobooks in bed or watching things on Netflix – I have just watched The Crown*. I also like listening to the radio. I like the radio programme:* More or Less *and listen to BBC Radio 4 – I get very bored with it, but I also like it because it tells me the time of the day and they have news on the hour and that makes me feel connected to the world. I know all the programmes now.*

I have to wait for everything, because I need carers for help with everything, even to put lypsil on. Sometimes I can get very impatient with the carers, especially when they don't understand me. I feel less patient now, but I always try to say please and thank you to them. They work hard and it never seems that there are enough of them.

I remember having music therapy and the song I wrote with the therapist. I remember music in Putney as well. I now have to do this on my own. I sing O Canada and God Save the Queen. I also say the Lord's Prayer every day. I do this to help me with my speaking. I remember that Tashi really loved the poem Tyger Tyger Burning Bright *by William Blake. Maybe I need to learn this some time. I am getting a bit better, but I want to get back to normal – or at least have the dizziness go away. I know I can talk a bit longer on FaceTime now – before I could only talk for a little bit on the phone before feeling very tired. Now I can talk for a little longer and that is very important to me, because it means I can still feel connected to the people I love.*

My hope for the future is that my family stay near me and come to visit as much as possible. But I know it's not fair. But I still want it. I also want to see my friends again and miss their visits. The thing that gives me joy is when my family talks to me on FaceTime and come to see me. I also talk to my Mum and brothers on Face-Time. I fear that I will be like this forever and I am still in my forties, so to live like this for a long time is difficult: I will be cold, hot and have to wait for people to help me for the rest of my life.

My dreams for Tashi are that she has the opportunities that I had: To go to university and that she can have a career that she likes. I just want Léa to be happy. I like to see her every week and I am very happy when she says that she loves me, because she's very honest.

Index